GREAT PRESIDENTIAL WIT

(... I Wish *I* Was in the Book)

★★★

BOB DOLE

A LISA DREW BOOK

A TOUCHSTONE BOOK
PUBLISHED BY SIMON & SCHUSTER
New York   London   Toronto   Sydney   Singapore

TOUCHSTONE
Rockefeller Center
1230 Avenue of the Americas
New York, NY 10020

First Touchstone Edition 2002

TOUCHSTONE and colophon are registered trademarks
of Simon & Schuster Inc.

For information regarding special discounts for bulk purchases,
please contact Simon & Schuster Special Sales at 1-800-456-6798 or
business@simonandschuster.com

DESIGNED BY ERICH HOBBING

Set in Berthold Baskerville

Manufactured in the United States of America

1   3   5   7   9   10   8   6   4   2

The Library of Congress has cataloged the Scribner edition as follows:
Dole, Robert, J., 1923–
Great presidential wit–I wish I was in the book / Bob Dole.
p. cm.
"A Lisa Drew book."
1. Presidents–United States–Biography–Anecdotes.
2. Presidents–United States–Humor. I. Title.
E176.1.D65 2001
973'.09'9–dc21   00-052632

ISBN 0-7432-0392-5
0-7432-1527-3 (Pbk)

To the American people,
who, through good times and bad
(and through good presidents and bad),
have never lost their sense
of humor.

ACKNOWLEDGMENTS

The irrepressible Will Rogers once said, "There's no trick to being a humorist when you have the whole government working for you." In that spirit, I want to thank all presidents—past and present—for the material they have provided for this book. I would also like to thank Lisa Drew, for her continuing support of this project, and Mel Berger, for helping to shepherd it along. I've also discovered that it's no trick to write a book on presidential humor when you are working with talented and funny people like Richard Norton Smith, Kerry Tymchuk, and Doug MacKinnon. My thanks to them for making this effort enjoyable and entertaining.

CONTENTS

INTRODUCTION:

BACKBONES AND FUNNY BONES

> Any man who has the job I have and didn't have a sense of humor wouldn't still be here.
>
> —HARRY TRUMAN

In listing qualifications for the presidency, the Constitution is as spare as it is specific. One must be at least thirty-five years of age, native born, and "a Resident within the United States" for at least fourteen years. That's it. Nothing about political judgment, educational background, oratorical skills, vision, or administrative talents. The Founders left it to posterity—and the professors—to fill in these and other blanks. A year ago C-SPAN invited historians to rank America's presidents, the latest in a never-ending series of academic polls gauging the men who have filled the nation's highest office. Not surprisingly, this rarefied electorate chose to emphasize such weighty criteria as economic management, political skills, international affairs, and the pursuit of social justice.

But there is another, less obvious element of presidential leadership. Second only to backbone, every president requires a funny bone. Certainly our most successful chief executives have exhibited both. Among these was Franklin D. Roosevelt. "The overwhelming majority of Americans are possessed of two great qualities," said FDR, "a sense of humor and a sense of proportion." In truth, they are one and the same. The greatest of leaders are not only able to laugh, they can laugh at themselves.

Most of the time, anyway. These days you can't swing a dead cat without hitting some historical pundit who has every presi-

11

dent neatly pigeonholed. But imagine if the roles were reversed. For years politicians have entertained Walter Mitty–ish fantasies about turning the table on our scholarly judges. (What *would* Chester Arthur think of Arthur Schlesinger Jr.?)

In the pages that follow I offer up my own, admittedly unscientific, attempt to assess, or reassess, America's presidents as humorists. They fall into eight categories:

1. *A Class by Themselves* (Lincoln, Reagan, Franklin Roosevelt, Theodore Roosevelt)
2. *Yankee Wits* (Coolidge, Kennedy)
3. *Plain Speaker, Tall Tales, and a Poker Face* (Truman, Lyndon Johnson, Hoover)
4. *Classroom Humorists* (Wilson, Garfield)
5. *Funnier Than the Average President* (Bush, Taft, John Adams, Washington, Jefferson, Clinton)
6. *And You Always Thought They Were Dull* (Eisenhower, Ford, Hayes, McKinley, Carter)
7. *Stick-in-the-Mud* (Grant, Monroe, Nixon, Tyler, Jackson, Arthur, John Quincy Adams, Andrew Johnson, Madison, Cleveland, Polk)
8. *The Joke's on Them* (Taylor, Harding, Van Buren, Buchanan, William Henry Harrison, Pierce, Benjamin Harrison, Fillmore)

At the top of the heap (and it should be remembered that this ranking still represents a "historical snapshot" and is a movable list that could continually change based upon the humor or lack thereof of the next occupant of the Oval Office) I place Abraham Lincoln, Ronald Reagan, and the two Roosevelts. By most accounts they are also among the most effective of chief executives. Coincidence? I don't think so. For occupants of the world's most stressful job, laughter is an emotional safety valve. "I laugh because I must not cry," said Lincoln during the darkest days of his war-ravaged presidency, in words that could have been echoed by FDR during World War II. The fact that they *could* laugh under such circumstances confirmed their essential humanity amidst the most inhuman pressures. And given the acknowledged recuperative benefits of humor, Ronald Reagan's wit may have done more than charm a nation—it may also have sped his recovery from a would-be assassin's bullet.

Nor is the presence of Franklin Pierce, Benjamin Harrison, and Millard Fillmore in the ranks of White House failures entirely unrelated to their joyless outlook. Don't get me wrong. Fillmore's been good for many a chuckle over the years. It's just that most of the laughter has come at his expense. In this he is hardly alone. Writing in the 1930s, Irwin "Ike" Hoover, who as chief usher had known every chief executive from the second Harrison through the second Roosevelt, portrayed the White House as a pretty grim place.

"How few presidents laugh heartily," wrote Hoover. "Taft was the exception. Harrison, Cleveland, McKinley, Wilson, Coolidge, Hoover—never more than a smile. Roosevelt forced himself into a laugh occasionally and Harding would break the rule once in a while. The extremes were Taft and Hoover. The latter never laughed aloud."

To be fair to President Hoover, the Great Depression was no laugh riot. Neither was the earlier depression with which Grover Cleveland had to contend, the Spanish-American War, which confronted McKinley, or the First World War, which overtook Woodrow Wilson. Yet in spite of—or perhaps because of—such demands, each of these presidents sought refuge in laughter. In fact, as readers are about to discover, Ike Hoover's claims don't always bear up under scrutiny. Woodrow Wilson could be downright risqué, Herbert Hoover turns out to be anything but the dour recluse depicted in most history books, and "Silent" Calvin Coolidge could just as easily have been "Sarcastic" Calvin Coolidge.

In *The Devil's Dictionary,* Ambrose Bierce defined the presidency as "the greased pig in the field game of American politics." Few of the contestants took themselves as seriously as the historians who pass judgment on their performance in office. Much as it goes against conventional wisdom, John Adams was a sharp-eyed satirist. Vast, placid William Howard Taft possessed a healthy sense of the ridiculous. And a generation after his death,

Harry Truman remains a bracing alternative to Washington pomposity. Indeed, I have spiced up these pages with some of Mr. Truman's observations about his fellow presidents. Like most of his comments, they do not lack for viewpoint.

"If I Didn't Laugh, I Should Die"

The United States is probably the only country on earth that puts the pursuit of happiness right after life and liberty among our God-given rights. Laughter and liberty go well together. So do humor and perspective, especially where human frailties are concerned. "It has been my experience," said Abraham Lincoln, "that folks who have no vices generally have very few virtues."

Nothing deflates pretense like a well-timed one-liner. Take the case of Lincoln's Springfield law partner, William Herndon. As effusive as his colleague was closemouthed, Herndon delivered a characteristically fulsome description of Niagara Falls just a few days after Lincoln had chanced to see this natural wonder with his own eyes. Herndon in full flight could be something of a natural wonder himself. He pulled out all the stops to convey the visual splendors of the foaming torrent, the roar of the rapids, and the sublime majesty of a rainbow permanently suspended above the Niagara gorge.

Exhausting his vocabulary of praise, the younger man finally asked Lincoln exactly what about the experience had made the deepest impression on him.

"The thing that struck me most forcibly when I saw the Falls," said Lincoln, "was, where in the world did all that water come from?"

It's hard to believe, but there was a time in American politics when candidates thought up their own sound bites. No one was better at this than Lincoln. After his perennial rival, Stephen A. Douglas, called him two-faced, Lincoln turned to his audience and drawled, "I leave it to you. If I had another face, do you think I would wear this one?" Not surprisingly, Douglas complained that every one of Lincoln's jokes "seems like a whack upon my back."

According to B. A. Botkin, a scholar of American folklore, the Great Emancipator "raised the wisecrack to the level of scripture." At the same time, it must be said of Lincoln's frontier humor that it is closer in style to Mark Twain than to Noël Coward. In September 1862, the embattled president prefaced a cabinet discussion over the proposed Emancipation Proclamation by reading a slightly gamy passage from Artemus Ward's *A High-Handed Outrage at Utica*. As the starchy statesmen around him squirmed in discomfort, Lincoln recounted an attack upon a waxen figure of Judas in a re-creation of the Last Supper.

"Judas Iscariot can't show himself in Utiky with impunerty by a darn site!" cries Ward's unlikely hero.

Glancing up from his book, Lincoln observed a distinct lack of amusement on his colleagues' faces. "Why don't you laugh, gentlemen?" he asked. "If I didn't laugh, I should die, and you need this medicine as much as I do." It's a bipartisan prescription, applicable to every occupant of 1600 Pennsylvania Avenue, but especially to history's favorites. As a boy Theodore Roosevelt watched Lincoln's funeral procession pass beneath the window of his New York brownstone. He developed a lifelong case of hero worship for the martyred president.

TR's own zest for life was legendary. Before a group of student athletes he expressed his guiding philosophy: "Don't flinch. Don't foul. And hit the line hard." Yet for all his triumphs, the first Roosevelt was no stranger to tragedy. He lost both his wife and his mother on the same terrible day. He saw his youngest son fall victim to enemy fire in the First World War. His political star dimmed after he left the White House. He lost as many elections as he won. But this apostle of the strenuous life never lost his sense of humor. Like Lincoln, TR used laughter as an antidote to tears.

Supplying a constant source of entertainment, the Roosevelt brood included five children and numerous pets. Characteristically, the president himself delighted in what he called Quentin's snake adventure. It seems that his youngest son had collected several snakes near the family estate on Long Island. One of the creatures escaped; the others made their way to the nation's capital, where they terrorized government officials, to the huge amusement of the Roosevelts.

"I was discussing certain matters with the attorney general," the president explained matter-of-factly, "and the snakes were easily deposited in my lap. The king snake, by the way, although most friendly with Quentin, had just been making a resolute effort to devour one of the smaller snakes. As Quentin and his menagerie were an interruption to my interview with the Department of Justice, I suggested that he go into the next room, where four congressmen were drearily waiting until I should be at leisure. I thought that he and his snakes would probably enliven their waiting time. He at once fell in with the suggestion and rushed up to the congressmen with the assurance that he would there find kindred spirits. They at first thought the snakes were wooden ones, and there was some perceptible recoil when they realized that they were alive. The last I saw of Quentin, one congressman was gingerly helping him off with his jacket, so as to let the snake crawl out of the upper end of the sleeve."

This is one way to impress lawmakers. In my own experience, presidents generally regard the *other* end of Pennsylvania Avenue as a snake pit.

ODD COUPLES

Granted, measuring the presidents as humorists plays havoc with more conventional rankings. But what is more subversive than laughter? There is no sharper weapon than one's tongue (believe me, I've cut myself from time to time). For the whimsical, humor can serve as a verbal sword; for the shy or repressed, it can afford a shield against those who might otherwise come too close or probe too deeply.

Which brings us to those Yankee wits, Calvin Coolidge and John F. Kennedy. Besides their New England roots, they would seem to have as much in common as chalk and (cheddar) cheese. In fact, both used laughter to puncture self-importance. Reading about one of his White House aides who had been described in a newspaper account as "coruscatingly" brilliant, Kennedy gibed, "Those guys should never forget, fifty thousand votes the other way and we'd all be coruscatingly stupid."

Soon after his confrontation with the steel industry in 1961, Kennedy said he was visited by a well-known businessman who seemed decidedly pessimistic about the economy. He tried to reassure his visitor by saying, "Why, if I weren't president, I'd be buying stock myself."

"If you weren't president," the businessman replied, "so would I."

Compared to the charismatic Kennedy, Coolidge was more arch than conservative. Denied the usual political gifts, Coolidge created a public persona that held the world at bay while allowing him to indulge a razor-edged humor. All his life, the man stereotyped as Silent Cal battled paralyzing shyness. As a boy in Vermont, the sound of strangers being entertained by his parents in the kitchen had frozen him in his tracks. For the adult Coolidge, an introvert in an extrovert's profession, greeting their counterparts on the campaign trail required an act of will. In time he conquered his crippling reserve, "but every time I meet a stranger," Coolidge acknowledged, "I've got to go through the old kitchen door back home, and it's not easy."

His reticence was matched by his canniness. Over the years, Coolidge developed his silent act into a running joke, a fierce, funny individuality cackling at pretense. His way of putting down political panhandlers was as distinctive as the broad *a* of his Yankee dialect. When a congresswoman from Illinois laid siege to the White House hoping to secure a federal judgeship for a prominent Chicagoan of Polish descent, she arranged for a group of Polish-Americans to lobby the president in person. Ushered into the executive office, the group shuffled its feet uncomfortably as a stony-faced Coolidge stared at the floor. After what seemed like an eternity, the president at last broke his silence.

"Mighty fine carpet there."

Both relieved and expectant, the delegation gladly nodded its concurrence.

"New one," said Coolidge. "Cost a lot of money."

At this, his guests smiled more appreciatively.

"She wore out the old one trying to get you a judge."

Thus did Coolidge enjoy a laugh on his less whimsical contemporaries. Historians, not noted for their whimsy, have by and large missed the joke. Calvin, We Hardly Knew Ye.

Sooner or later, all presidents make us laugh. Not all make us laugh *with them*. Much of what follows can best be categorized as insult humor—some aimed by, the rest at, the man in the White House. Contemporary journalists, for example, thought Coolidge funny in a perverse kind of way. The Sage of Baltimore, H. L. Mencken, went so far as to define democracy as "that system of government under which the people, having 35,717,342 native born adult whites to choose from, including thousands who are handsome and many who are wise, pick out the Hon. Mr. Coolidge to be the head of state. It is as if a hungry man, set before a banquet prepared by master cooks and covering a table an acre in area, should turn his back upon the feast and stay his stomach by catching and eating flies."

Mencken was even rougher on Coolidge's predecessor, dismissing the amiable Warren G. Harding as "a tinhorn politician with the manner of a rural corn doctor and the mien of a ham actor." An equal-opportunity abuser, Mencken labeled the high-minded Woodrow Wilson "The Archangel Woodrow." Urbane and polished, Wilson ranks high in any listing of amusing presidents. Few readers, I suspect, would say as much for his fellow onetime college president, James Garfield. Think again. Together this unlikely pair make up a category I call "Classroom Humorists."

Just above Wilson and Garfield is a grouping entitled "Plain Speaking, Tall Tales, and a Poker Face," encompassing Presidents Harry Truman, Lyndon Johnson, and Herbert Hoover, all of whom were generously endowed with comic sensibilities. The irrepressible Liz Carpenter, who served as Lady Bird Johnson's press secretary during her years as first lady, recalls an occasion when White House speechwriters sent President Johnson a highfalutin text replete with quotations from Aristotle.

"Aristotle!" snorted LBJ. "Those folks don't know who the hell Aristotle is." Johnson decided to credit Aristotle's words to somebody more familiar, and he inserted the phrase "as my dear old daddy used to say to me . . ."

Hoover, too, used humor to cut to the point. When his wife invited an African-American woman to be her guest at the White House in the summer of 1929, it touched off an uproar in some quarters. Incredible as it seems, no such courtesy had ever been extended before then. A few members of the Texas legislature even demanded the president's impeachment.

More amused than angered, Hoover reassured the first lady that she had done the morally correct thing. Besides, he told her, "one of the chief advantages of orthodox religion is that it provides a hot hell for the Texas legislature."

MAKING WASHINGTON SMILE

Another rung of the ladder is entitled "Funnier Than the Average President," and is reserved for presidents who exhibited a healthier sense of humor than most presidents, but who didn't quite make what my friend David Letterman would call my "top ten." This list begins with George Bush and ends with Bill Clinton. In between are some of America's earliest presidents, who appear to modern audiences as lifeless as the marble statues with which they are commemorated. It's not really their fault. In an age more attuned to Marilyn Monroe than James Monroe, time itself works against them. If satire closes on Saturday night, then the shelf life of most political humor rivals that of overripe bananas. Granted, no Catskills comic could have written the Declaration of Independence, but what brought a smile to Jefferson's lips is unlikely to amuse the *There's Something About Mary* generation.

Topicality aside, there is another reason our Founding Fathers appear so forbidding. Early historians felt the need to deify these paragons whose job was to invest a radically new, untested system of government with as much dignity as they could summon. At the Constitutional Convention in Philadelphia, James Madison allegedly made a bet with New York's Gouverneur Morris. Madison promised to treat his colleague to a handsome dinner if

Morris would go up to Washington, slap him on the back, and address him by his first name. Morris accepted the wager, so the story goes, only to be rewarded by an arctic blast from the presiding officer. Morris won the dinner, while vowing never again to cross the line of familiarity with the majestic Washington.

There's nothing very funny about the story, unless you wonder why anyone would name their child Gouverneur. Like most of his fellow demigods in periwigs, however, Washington *could* be amusing. Soon after returning home from the convention, for example, he hired a gardener for his Mount Vernon estate. Washington drew up a contract with a hard-drinking candidate, after solemnly binding the man to perform his duties sober for one year "if allowed four dollars at Christmas, with which to be drunk four days and four nights; two dollars at Easter, to affect the same purpose; two dollars at Whitsuntide, to be drunk for two days, a dram in the morning and a drink of grog at dinner and at noon."

Everyone's heard of Washington's dentures. Has anyone ever seen them? For that matter, have you ever seen a smile cross the lips of all those other pre–Civil War presidents whose idealized portraits are so unrelentingly serious? Blame it on the distorting lens of primitive photography. The earliest cameras required too long an exposure to result in anything other than the tight-lipped, grim visages captured in daguerreotypes.

Making things worse was the fact that presidential speech and joke writers and priggish editors who insisted on cleaning up presidential language before sharing it with posterity weren't "invented" until the twentieth century. As farmers or plantation owners, most of our early presidents were accustomed to barnyard references. Yet when the grandson of John Adams set out to publish his distinguished ancestor's correspondence, he was careful to delete "low" remarks, many of them humorous and all of them revealing.

From George to George . . . when George Bush published a generous sampling of his most personal correspondence in 1999, it came as a revelation to many readers. Typical was this Bush diary entry for November 7, 1987: "Brandon, Iowa. A tiny little town. More people in the middle of the little town than lived in the town. They came in from everywhere. The firemen, dressed in yellow coats, holding the crowd back. Young kids, banners, homemade signs welcoming the Vice President. I go into the Brandon Feedstore, and just before walking in I was shaking hands with all the people and an older woman said to me, 'You look younger than I thought.' I said, 'A lot of people say, taller.' She said, 'No, I say a lot younger.' I said, 'Well, I'm sixty-three.' She said, 'No s---?' Everybody heard her. All of the people standing next to her looked shocked, looked kind of held back. I laughed and then they laughed like mad. It was absolutely fantastic. One of the great moments in my life politically."

Soon after succeeding George Bush in the White House, Bill Clinton confided at a Democratic fund-raising dinner, "I used to have a sense of humor, but they told me it wasn't presidential, so I had to quit."

Yeah, sure. Clinton, who often called upon Hollywood acquaintances to pen his best lines, understood that no modern president can forgo the weapon of laughter, among the most formidable in any politician's arsenal. And President Clinton was hardly the sort to embrace unilateral disarmament. Of Warren Christopher, his famously buttoned-down secretary of state, Clinton said that he was "the only man ever to eat presidential M&M's on Air Force One with a knife and fork."

At the 2000 White House Correspondents' Association dinner, a president mindful of his legacy was bold enough to joke about the scandals of his administration. "You know, the clock is running down on the Republicans in Congress, too. I feel for them. I do," said Clinton. "They've only got seven more months to investigate me. That's a lot of pressure. So little time, so many unanswered questions. For example, over the last few months, I've lost ten pounds. Where did they go? Why haven't I produced them to the independent counsel? How did some of them manage to wind up on Tim Russert [the host of NBC's *Meet the Press*]?"

EGGS AND BISCUITS

Dwight Eisenhower and Gerald Ford, often underrated as presidents, are also underrated as humorists. They head up a category entitled "And You Always Thought They Were Dull." Ike is a hero of mine, not least because he recognized humor as a vital part "of getting along with people, of getting things done." What's more, he made no attempt to conceal his geographical loyalties. Although born in Texas, where his father had gone to find employment on the railroad, Ike returned to Abilene, Kansas, when he was two years old. For the rest of his life, therefore, Eisenhower considered himself a Kansan. As he put it, "A chicken may hatch her eggs in the oven, but they're still not biscuits."

He wasn't always so succinct. Students of the Eisenhower presidency have theorized that he sometimes deliberately scrambled his syntax in an effort to divert reporters hot on the trail of a story. Warned by his press secretary, Jim Hagerty, of a politically sensitive question sure to be raised, Ike replied, "Don't worry, Jim. If it comes up, I'll just confuse them."

You be the judge. At a 1954 press conference, the president was asked, "If you find there is no need at the session of Congress for changes in the program, would you suggest further amendments?"

"Indeed I will," replied Eisenhower. "I don't believe I have yet gotten stupid enough to believe I am so smart that I know all of the answers in advance."

Whether or not longevity is the best revenge, Gerald Ford illustrates that ex-presidents often discover a sense of humor they rarely exhibited in office. Appearing before the National Press Club on the eve of the Democratic convention that nominated Vice President Gore for president, Ford needled the vice president over his less than scintillating speaking style. "Al Gore went to the beach the other day to give a speech on the environment," said Ford. "The tide went out and never came back." Some of President Ford's golf shots may have gone astray, but if the worst thing the press can accuse you of is bumping your head—well, history will be much kinder than Dan Rather. Take it from one who fell off that stage in Chico.

Ford's successor, Jimmy Carter, has also displayed hidden reserves of laughter as an ex-president. Typical is this story from his book *Living Faith*. As he tells it, "this fellow died and went to heaven. When he got there, he was met by St. Peter and an angel. And St. Peter asked him, 'Tell me something about yourself.' And he said, 'I got a doctorate from a major university; I've been very successful in my business life; I've been active in my church—taught Sunday school even—and feel I'm very well qualified.'

"St. Peter said, 'What have you ever done for anybody else?' And the fellow thought for a moment and said, 'Back in the Depression years, a group of hoboes came by my house, and Ma fixed a bunch of sandwiches, and I gave them to them. And even in depressed dollars, that was worth at least fifty cents.'

"St. Peter said, 'Have you done anything more recently?'

"And the fellow said, 'As a matter of fact, just last year, my neighbor's house burned down. I looked around my back porch among some old furniture, and I found a little table and I took it over and gave it to him. That was also worth about fifty cents.'

"St. Peter said to the angel, 'Go down to earth and see if his story is true.'

"So the angel went down, came back, and said, 'Yes, sir, what he said is absolutely right. What should we do with him?'

"St. Peter said, 'Give him his dollar back and tell him to go to hell.'"

VICTIMS OF HISTORY

Now comes the part sure to keep this book out of several presidential birthplace gift shops—listing the chief executives who may have had many qualities, but a sense of humor wasn't high on the list. This list includes John Quincy Adams, one of the brightest men ever to serve as president. In the history books Adams languishes in the shadow of Andrew Jackson, the frontier hero and popular champion who gave his name to an age. "I was not formed to shine in company," Adams confided to his diary, "nor to be delighted with it." In modern jargon, he didn't feel our pain. On the other hand, he could write English with one hand while translating Greek with the other.

Adams's greatest gift, however, was for running down his opponents. Of one particularly obnoxious rival, he declared, "His face is livid, gaunt his whole body, his breath is green with gall; his tongue drips poison."

And they said *I* had a sharp tongue.

James Madison may be another victim of history. One Philadelphia delegate wrote of the little man from Virginia that he had "a remarkably sweet temper." A female visitor to his Virginia estate called the fourth president a great conversationalist and storyteller. "Every sentence he spoke was worthy of being written down," she told friends. Unfortunately, she didn't write any of them down. Nor has anyone else. On the other hand, Madison's historical stature has hardly suffered from his dry-as-dust image. It's one thing to appear on Comedy Central with Jon Stewart, something else to be the Father of the Constitution.

All of which goes to show that not every successful president requires the ability to go *mano a mano* with Leno or Letterman. Consider the man whose diplomatic achievements far outweighed his joke-telling abilities. Come to think of it, there must have been times when Richard Nixon looked upon Watergate as a bad joke. President Nixon and I have much in common. We both grew up amidst rural privation. We both served in World War II. We both served in the House and the Senate. Of course, there are some differences as well. That's why we call him President Nixon.

Nixon, of course, had more reincarnations than Shirley MacLaine. One thing about him never changed. In her marvelous biography of her mother, Julie Eisenhower recalls an occasion on which Pat Nixon expressed amazement at her husband's perseverance in the face of criticism.

"I just get up every morning to confound my enemies," said Nixon.

Nixon probably confounded famed JFK speechwriter Ted

Sorensen, when the two crossed paths in Chicago soon after Kennedy's inaugural address. "I wish I had said some of those things," Nixon said.

"What part?" asked the proud Sorensen, who had written the speech. "That part about 'Ask not what your country can do for you . . .'?"

"No," explained Nixon. "The part that starts, 'I do solemnly swear. . . .' "

THE JOKE'S ON THEM

Then, we come to my final category—eight well-intentioned, deservedly obscure leaders run over by history or reduced to the status of academic punching bag. Neither Martin Van Buren nor Millard Fillmore went gently into that good night. Each man attempted a comeback as a third-party candidate for the White House, Van Buren on the Free Soil ticket, Fillmore as a Know-Nothing (I'm not making this up. In 1856 there was a Know-Nothing party. These days many voters regard this as a bipartisan affiliation).

I try to keep their sobering examples in mind when asked about the possibility of again seeking the presidency. Then I repeat something attributed to W. C. Fields: "If at first you don't succeed, try, try again. Then quit. No use being a damn fool about it."

Can you imagine Zachary Taylor saying that?

What follows is my own admittedly unscientific attempt to rate America's presidents as humorists, the "Dole Poll of Presidential Wit and Humor" (fans of bipartisanship take note: five of those I rank in the top ten are Republicans and five are Democrats):

1. Abraham Lincoln: *Our greatest president was also our funniest president.*
2. Ronald Reagan: *His actor's timing never failed him.*
3. Franklin D. Roosevelt: *His wit helped him—and America—survive a depression and a world war.*

4. Theodore Roosevelt: *Lived life to the fullest—and that included lots of laughter.*

5. Calvin Coolidge: *A man of few words—but many of them were funny.*

6. John Kennedy: *His press conferences were often the wittiest show on TV.*

7. Harry Truman: *A plainspoken Midwesterner who told it like it was—is there any wonder why I like this guy?*

8. Lyndon Johnson: *A master of Texas tall tales. You laughed at his jokes—or else.*

9. Herbert Hoover: *Beneath the Quaker exterior beat the heart of a comedian.*

10. Woodrow Wilson: *Proof that intellectuals can also be funny.*

11. James Garfield: *One of the best orators of his time—and not a bad humorist, either.*

12. George Bush: *He could never take himself too seriously because he was blessed with America's wittiest first lady.*

13. William Howard Taft: *Resembled Santa Claus in girth and in jolliness.*

14. John Adams: *Often cranky and full of insults—an eighteenth-century Don Rickles.*

15. George Washington: *First in peace, first in war, but middle of the pack when it came to humor.*

16: Thomas Jefferson: *He gets credit for guaranteeing all Americans "life, liberty, and the pursuit of happiness."*

17. Bill Clinton: *Blessed with great speaking ability and talented joke writers.*

18. Dwight Eisenhower: *Only president to write a best-selling book of his favorite anecdotes.*

19. Gerald Ford: *His sense of humor, like his presidency, has been underrated.*

20. Rutherford Hayes: *His wife, "Lemonade Lucy," ran a dry White House. He matched it with a dry sense of humor.*

21. William McKinley: *Teddy Roosevelt carried the big stick. McKinley spoke softly.*

22. Jimmy Carter: *His smile was famous, his jokes weren't.*

23. Ulysses Grant: *Was more successful and funnier as a soldier than as a president.*

24. James Monroe: *Anyone who presided over the "Era of Good Feelings" had to have had some sense of humor.*

25. Richard Nixon: *Those weren't jokes that were deleted from the Watergate tapes.*

26. John Tyler: *Harry Truman described him as a "contrary old son of a bitch." Enough said.*

27. Andrew Jackson: *Guns—and not words—were his weapon of choice.*

28. Chester Arthur: *Often depicted as a high-living socialite. His reform of the Civil Service System, however, gave future presidents much more time to laugh.*

29. John Quincy Adams: *Described himself as "reserved, cold, and austere." Obviously, no laugh riot.*

30. Andrew Johnson: *Destined to remain forever in Lincoln's shadow.*

31. James Madison: *Father of the Constitution didn't produce many laughs.*

32. Grover Cleveland: *The only president to be nonfunny in nonconsecutive terms.*

33. James Polk: *A workaholic who never had time to laugh.*

34. Zachary Taylor: *One of the original grumpy old men.*

35. Warren Harding: *Too few jokes, too many mistresses.*

36. Martin Van Buren: *His nickname was "o.k." but his sense of humor wasn't.*

37. James Buchanan: *Few presidents came to office with more experience—or less of a sense of humor.*

38. William Henry Harrison: *If he had joked more and spoken less, he might not have caught pneumonia during his inaugural address, which led to his death a month later.*

39. Franklin Pierce: *Granite State native also had a granite face.*

40. Benjamin Harrison: *"Cold-blooded" and "icy" were terms his friends used to describe him.*

41. Millard Fillmore: *Our thirteenth president was unlucky in the wit and humor department.*

A Class by Themselves

#1 ABRAHAM LINCOLN

"I've endured a great deal of ridicule without much malice," Lincoln once observed, "and have received a great deal of kindness not quite free from ridicule."

In the 1830s, while living in New Salem, Lincoln joined the local militia and served in the Black Hawk War. Mocking himself as well as his country's habit of entrusting supreme power to military men, Lincoln later joked that the only blood he had spilled in defense of his country was to mosquitoes.

Lincoln had a natural gift for sarcasm, which he learned to control. Nevertheless, it occasionally spilled out. Of one long-winded orator, he observed, "He can compress the most words into the smallest ideas of any man I ever met."

"When I hear a man preach," said Lincoln, "I like to see him act as if he were fighting bees." Such irreverence occasionally landed young Lincoln in hot water. One Springfield editor went so far as to rebuke the rising politician for "his assumed clownishness." Lincoln couldn't help himself; frontier wit bubbled up from within his tall frame. One of his favorite stories concerned the backwoods meetinghouse in which an itinerant preacher held forth. The minister wore old-fashioned baggy pantaloons, with no suspenders, and a shirt fastened at the collar with one button. He began his sermon by announcing his text: "I am the Christ, whom I shall represent today."

About this time a small blue lizard ran up one of the preacher's legs. The preacher grew desperate. Without pausing for breath, he undid the single button holding up his trousers. Immediately the offending lizard crawled up the preacher's back. This time he unfastened the button holding his shirt, even while repeating, "I am the Christ, whom I shall represent today." One can imagine the reaction of those in the pews. Amidst the shocked silence, one elderly lady slowly stood up and pointed a finger toward the man in the pulpit.

"I just want to say that if you represent Jesus Christ, sir, then I'm done with the Bible."

A Springfield neighbor looked out the window one day and saw Lincoln carrying his two sons, Willie and Tad. The boys were shouting at each other and punching the air.

"What's wrong?" said Lincoln's neighbor.

"Just what's the matter with the whole world," replied Lincoln. "I've got three walnuts and each wants two."

Of his perennial rival Stephen A. Douglas, candidate Lincoln said that Douglas's supporters "have seen in his round, jolly, fruitful face, post offices, land offices, marshalships, and cabinet appointments, charge-ships and foreign missions, bursting out in wonderful exuberance."

Lincoln made light of Douglas's arguments, what he called "a specious and fantastic arrangement of words, by which a man can prove a horse chestnut to be a chestnut horse."

The famed Lincoln–Douglas debates of 1858 did much to establish the rawboned Illinois lawyer as a national figure. Though both men went at each other hammer and tongs, Lincoln never lost his sense of humor. At the town of Galesburg, he handed his long cloak to a friend, remarking, "Hold this while I stone Stephen."

In these same debates, Stephen Douglas thought he had scored a point when he recalled his first meeting with Lincoln—at a time when Lincoln was a storekeeper in New Salem, selling whiskey and cigars. "Mr. Lincoln was a very good bartender!" said Douglas.

"What Mr. Douglas has said is true enough," Lincoln replied. "I did keep a grocery, and I did sell cotton, candles, and cigars, and sometimes whiskey. I remember in those days that Mr. Douglas was one of my best customers. Many a time have I stood on one side of the counter and sold whiskey to Mr. Douglas on the other side, but the difference between us now is this: I have left my side of the counter, but Mr. Douglas still sticks to his as tenaciously as ever."

How's this for psychological insight? "Tact," said Lincoln, "is the ability to describe others as they see themselves."

Lincoln's wife, Mary, was famously interested in spiritualism. The author of a book on the subject sent a copy to the president.

Someone asked Lincoln his opinion of the volume. "Well," said Lincoln, "for those who like that sort of thing, I should think that it's just about the sort of thing they would like."

Lincoln was one of the most successful attorneys of his time. Part of his success was due to his humor. Remarking on a wordy document drafted by a lawyer, Lincoln said, "It's like the lazy preacher who used to write long sermons, and the explanation was, he got to writing and was too lazy to stop."

At the 1860 Republican convention in Chicago, Lincoln's managers followed the time-honored practice of dangling cabinet jobs before prospective supporters. Although the candidate himself had ordered them to "make no contracts that will bind me," campaign manager David Davis, a realist in such matters, dismissed such instructions out of hand. "Lincoln ain't here and don't know what we have to meet!"

Among those with whom Davis was forced to deal was Simon Cameron, a sticky-fingered senator from Pennsylvania who would soon demonstrate his ineptitude as secretary of war. Horrified that Honest Abe would align himself with so unsavory a boss, Cameron's sworn enemy Thaddeus Stevens hurried to warn Lincoln before it was too late.

"You don't mean to say you think Cameron would steal?" asked Lincoln.

"No," said Stevens, "I don't think he would steal a red-hot stove."

Lincoln found this so amusing that he couldn't keep from repeating the story–to Cameron–who, not surprisingly, demanded a retraction. In good time a red-faced Stevens appeared at the White House.

"Mr. Lincoln, why did you tell Cameron what I said to you?"

"I thought it was a good joke and didn't think it would make him mad."

"Well, he is very mad and made me promise to retract," sputtered Stevens. "I will now do so. I believe I told you he would *not* steal a red-hot stove. I now take that back."

A rather haughty female visitor accosted Lincoln at a White House reception and demanded that he give her son a colonel's commission, not as a favor, but as a right. "Sir, my grandfather fought at Lexington," she informed the president. "My uncle was the only man who did not run away at Bladensburg. My father fought at New Orleans, sir, and my husband was killed at Monterrey."

"Madame," Lincoln replied, "your family has done enough for the country. It is time to give somebody else a chance."

One afternoon Lincoln found on his desk a heartrending appeal for a pardon, unsupported by the usual sheaf of letters from influential sponsors.

"What," asked the president, "has this man no friends?"

The adjutant at Lincoln's side assured him that the man hadn't a one.

"Then I will be his friend," said Lincoln. He signed the pardon.

A pair of Tennessee women called at the White House one day seeking the release of their rebel husbands from a Northern prison. One of them argued for the release because her husband was a deeply religious man.

"Madame," said Lincoln, "you say your husband is a religious man. Perhaps I am not a good judge of these things, but in my opinion the religion that makes men rebel and fight against a just government in defense of an unjust institution that makes slaves of men whom God made free is not the genuine article. The religion that reconciles men to the idea of eating their bread in the sweat of other men's faces is not the kind to get to heaven on."

Ultimately, Lincoln gave way in the face of the women's appeals—but not before he urged them to reexamine their own religious practices.

"True patriotism," observed Lincoln, "is more holy than false piety."

Poor generalship was the bane of Lincoln's presidency. One day, on learning that the enemy had captured a Union brigadier general and twelve army mules, Lincoln responded in character. "How unfortunate," he exclaimed. "Those *mules* cost us two hundred dollars apiece."

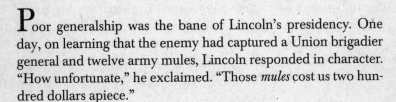

In December 1862 a crisis arose in Lincoln's cabinet. Senatorial critics egged on by Treasury Secretary Salmon P. Chase demanded that the president fire Secretary of State William Seward. At the ensuing showdown, thanks to Lincoln's adroit maneuvering, Chase was forced to take back much of what he had told the senators in secret. This left an embarrassed Chase no alternative but to tender his own resignation, something Seward had already offered. Lincoln was exultant. "Now, I can ride," he exclaimed, "I have a pumpkin in each end of my bag." As a matter of fact, he refused both resignations—having established his mastery over both men.

Lincoln once told a hotel waiter, "If this is coffee, please bring me some tea; but if this is tea, please bring me some coffee."

Lincoln frequently clashed with the sluggish General George B. McClellan. After the president ordered the general to keep him better informed of activities in the field, McClellan resorted to mockery, sending the following telegram to the White House.

> To President Abraham Lincoln
> Washington DC
> Have just captured six cows. What shall we do with them?
> George B. McClellan

Lincoln, not to be outdone, wired back:

> General George B. McClellan
> Army of the Potomac
> Milk them.
> A. Lincoln

Few presidents have been so beset by problems as Lincoln. When, in the darkest days of the Civil War, a delegation of prominent Bostonians came to the White House to voice their complaints, the president listened patiently before asking, "Do you remember that a few years ago Blondin walked across a tightrope stretched over the falls of Niagara?"

The men before him nodded their heads. Lincoln continued:

"Suppose that all the material values in this great country of ours, from the Atlantic to the Pacific—its wealth, its prosperity, its achievements in the present and its hopes for the future—could all have been concentrated and given to Blondin to carry over that awful crossing and that their preservation should have depended upon his ability to somehow get them across to the other side—and suppose that everything you yourself held dearest in the world, the safety of your family, and the security of your home, also depended upon his crossing.

"And suppose you had been on the shore when he was going over, as he was carefully feeling his way along and balancing his pole with all his most delicate skill over the thundering cataract. Would you have shouted to him, 'Blondin, a step to the right!' 'Blondin, a step to the left!' Or would you have stood there speechless and held your breath and prayed to the Almighty to guide and help him safely through the trial?"

The visiting delegation got the point. Silently they rose, gathered up their hats, and bid the president farewell.

In the autumn of 1863, beset as always by office seekers, Lincoln's physician told him that he was suffering from varioloid, a mild form of smallpox.

"Is it contagious?" asked the president.

"Very contagious," the doctor assured him.

Lincoln seemed oddly pleased. The doctor asked why. "There is one good thing about this," the president told him. "Now I have something I can give everybody."

At one critical juncture in the war, Lincoln was annoyed to receive in the mail a request for an autograph and a "sentiment" accompanying his signature.

"Dear Madame," he responded, "when you ask from a stranger that which is of interest only to yourself, always enclose a stamp. There's your sentiment, and here's my autograph. A. Lincoln."

Lincoln didn't pretend to be much of an authority on art. Once asked to give his opinion of a portrait that was anything but lifelike, Lincoln pronounced the painter to be a great artist indeed. Moreover, said Lincoln, "He observes the Lord's commandments."

Asked what he meant by that, Lincoln replied, "It seems to me that he hath not made to himself a likeness of anything that is in the heaven above, or that is in the earth beneath, or that is in the waters under the earth."

Lincoln professed indifference to his ancestry. "I don't know who my grandfather was," he once said. "I am much more concerned to know what his grandson will be."

Lincoln's old Illinois friend Jesse Dubois openly campaigned for a place in the cabinet. Unfortunately, said Lincoln, he needed a Methodist to balance the present slate. Asked to explain himself, the president said, "There's Seward who is an Episcopalian; Chase is an Episcopalian; Bates is an Episcopalian; and Stanton swears enough to be one."

Once, when the radical Senator Benjamin Wade of Ohio came to harangue the president, Lincoln tried putting him off with an amusing story.

"Yes, Mr. President," barked Wade, "it is nothing but anecdotes. I have heard enough of them. You are letting the country go to hell on anecdotes. We are not more than a mile from there now."

Now it was Lincoln's turn to interrupt.

"Mr. Wade," said the president, "that is just about the distance to the Capitol, isn't it?"

On another occasion the meddlesome Senator Wade tried to browbeat the president into removing General George B. McClellan from his command. But who, Lincoln asked, would then lead the Union armies?

"Why, anybody could," snorted Wade. "Certainly anybody could do a better job than McClellan."

"Wade," said Lincoln, "*anybody* will do for you, but not for me. I must have *somebody*."

At its worst, the tide of office seekers threatened to swamp even the war in Lincoln's priorities. A friend calling at the White House one day, and finding the president looking terribly weary and dispirited, asked, "What is the matter, Mr. Lincoln? Has anything gone wrong at the front?"

Lincoln smiled wanly. "No, it isn't the war. It's the post office at Brownsville, Missouri."

Lincoln was a frequent visitor to the telegraph office at the War Department, where he would go to a desk, open the drawer, and peruse a tall stack of dispatches from the front. On reaching the bottom of one such pile, he remarked, "Well, I guess I've got down to the raisins."

A clerk hearing this odd expression asked the president to explain it. Lincoln readily obliged by telling of the little girl out West who was sometimes inclined to eat too much. "One day she ate a good many more raisins than was good for her and followed them down with a quantity of other goodies. Sure enough, she got very sick. At last, the raisins began to come up. The little girl gasped, looked at her mother, and said, 'Well, I will be better now, for I have got down to the raisins.'"

At a White House reception, an elderly guest waved his hat and cried out, "Mr. President, I'm from up in New York State where we believe that God Almighty and Abraham Lincoln are going to save this country."

A smile played on Lincoln's face and he nodded. "My friend," said the president, "you're half-right."

In an especially bleak moment in his 1864 campaign for reelection, a friend bluntly asked the president whether he expected to win.

"Well," replied Lincoln, "I don't think I ever heard of any man being elected to an office unless someone was for him."

Nothing pained Lincoln so much as passing sentence on deserting soldiers. "I don't believe it will make a man any better to shoot him, while if we keep him alive, we may at least get some work out of him," the president explained in justification of his lenient policy. "You have no doubt heard the story of the soldier who was caught and asked why he had deserted. 'Well, Captain,' he said, 'it was not my fault. I have got just as brave a heart as Julius Caesar, but these legs of mine will always run away with me when the battle begins.'

"I have no doubt," continued Lincoln, "that is true of many a man who honestly meant to do his duty, but who was overcome by a physical fear greater than his will." Thereafter, Lincoln himself referred to his "leg cases."

When asked how he dealt with criticism from members of his own party, Lincoln said, "I feel on the subject as an old Illinois farmer once expressed himself while eating cheese. He was interrupted in the midst of his repast by the entrance of his son, who exclaimed, 'Hold on, Dad! There's bugs in the cheese!' The man kept on eating, saying, 'Never mind, Son. If they can stand it, I can.'"

When Lincoln was nominated for a second term in 1864, an ally told him that the only way he could lose would be if General Grant took Richmond and then decided to run for president himself. "Well," said Lincoln, "I feel very much like the man who, after a serious talk with his doctor, said he didn't want to die particularly, but if he had to die, that was precisely the disease he would like to die of."

After Lincoln's attorney general Edward Bates resigned in 1864, the cabinet was without Southerners, a serious liability in an election year. Indeed, said Lincoln, "If the twelve apostles were to be chosen nowadays, the interest of locality would have to be heeded."

Of all his burdens, none lay more heavily on Lincoln than the constant press of office seekers. Even here, however, he managed to see the humor of the situation, telling of a fellow who had come to the White House "asking for an appointment as a minister abroad. Finding he could not get that, he came down to some more modest position. Finally he asked to be made a tie-waiter. When he saw he could not get that, he asked me for an old pair of trousers. It is sometimes well to be humble."

To one obnoxious applicant for a post that had already been filled, Lincoln sent this telegraph: "What nation do you desire to be made quartermaster general of? This nation already has a quartermaster general."

One of Lincoln's most persistent callers came to him one day with the news that the chief of customs had just died. Could he possibly take his place? "It's fine with me if the undertaker doesn't mind," said Lincoln.

In a single sentence, Lincoln exposed not only the·evil of slavery, but the hypocrisy of its defenders, when he declared, "Whenever I hear anyone arguing for slavery, I feel a strong impulse to see it tried on him personally."

When an officer accused of embezzling $40 of federal funds appealed for leniency, explaining that in truth he had only stolen $30, Lincoln said he was reminded of the Indiana man who charged his neighbor's daughter with unseemly behavior for having three illegitimate children.

"Now, that's a lie," said the accused, "and I can prove it, for I only have two."

Worried friends advised the president that he should take greater precautions against potential assassination. To which Lincoln replied, "What is the use of putting up the bars when the fence is down all around?"

At the end of the war there was much debate concerning the whereabouts and punishment to be meted out to Jefferson Davis and other rebel leaders. For his own part, Lincoln would just as soon they escape to Canada or abroad. "When you have got an elephant by the hind leg and he is trying to run away," said the president, "it's best to let him run."

#2 RONALD REAGAN

A master of the one-liner, Reagan portrayed Washington as "the only city where sound travels faster than light."

"Politics is not a bad profession," acknowledged the citizen politician. "If you succeed, there are many rewards; if you disgrace yourself, you can always write a book."

Reagan delighted in telling of the young cub reporter whose first assignment was to go out to the senior citizens' home, where a man was celebrating his ninety-fifth birthday. "To what do you attribute your longevity?" the reporter asked.

The elderly man said, "I don't drink, I don't smoke, I don't run around with wild women." Just then there was a terrible crashing noise upstairs, and the kid says, "What's that?" And the ninety-five-year-old replied, "Oh, that's my father. He's drunk again."

At a time of rising inflation, then-Governor Reagan asked an audience, "Do you remember back in the days when you thought that nothing could replace the dollar? Today it practically has!"

Reagan was forever having fun at the expense of bureaucrats, including those he imagined might have rewritten the Ten Commandments along the following lines . . .

"Thou shalt not, unless you feel strongly to the contrary, or for the following stated exceptions, see paragraphs 1–10, subsection a."

Even the Great Communicator had his off days. Reagan once addressed a large and distinguished audience in Mexico City. When he finished, he sat down to scattered, decidedly unenthusiastic applause. His embarrassment grew when the next speaker, a representative of the Mexican government who addressed the crowd in Spanish, was interrupted repeatedly by applause and laughter. To hide his embarrassment, Reagan joined in the clapping—until the U.S. ambassador leaned over and said, "I wouldn't do that if I were you; he's interpreting your speech."

According to Reagan, "An economist is someone who sees something happen in practice and wonders if it'd work in theory."

Reagan told this one on St. Patrick's Day, 1987: "My dear father once told me of a fellow who walked into a saloon, pounded on the bar, and said in a loud voice, 'Show me an Irishman, and I'll show you a wimp.' And a six-and-a-half-foot Irishman stepped forward, rolling up his shirtsleeves as he did so, and said, 'I'm Irish.' The fellow said, 'Well, I'm a wimp.'"

Reagan was perpetually suspicious of Washington's tendency to tax and spend. He defined a taxpayer as "someone who works for the federal government but doesn't have to take a civil service examination."

Reagan could actually be quite acerbic when he chose. During the 1980 campaign, for example, he said that Jimmy Carter was supposed to go on *60 Minutes* and talk about his accomplishments, "but that would have left fifty-nine minutes to fill." On another occasion the president spoke of a mythical friend invited to a costume ball: "He slapped some egg on his face and went as a liberal economist."

Before a gathering of conservative activists, Reagan claimed that there were two unbalanced things in Washington—the budget and the liberals.

Reagan liked to tell a story originally related to him by Mikhail Gorbachev. It seems there was an interminable line outside a Moscow grocery store, shuffling forward at a snail's pace. An entire day went by, and those in line didn't seem any closer to the store's entrance than at the start of the day. Finally, one Muscovite had had it.

"It's all Gorbachev's fault," he shouted. "I'm going to go and kill Gorbachev." And he rushed away.

Twenty-four hours later, he returned, with a crestfallen look on his face.

"Well," someone asked him, "did you kill Gorbachev?"

"No," replied the man. "That line was twice as long."

"It's no secret that I wear a hearing aid," Reagan told the White House Correspondents' Dinner in April 1987. "Well, just the other day, all of a sudden, it went haywire. We discovered the KGB had put a listening device in my listening device."

Reagan loved relating stories shared by the Soviet people among themselves. One of them concerned the mandatory ten-year waiting period to buy an automobile, and the requirement that a purchaser pay a full decade in advance. As Reagan told it, "There was a young fellow there that had finally made it, and he was going through all the bureaus and agencies that he had to go through, and signing all the papers, and finally he got to the last agency where they put the stamp on it. Then he gave them his money, and they said, 'Come back in ten years and get your car.'

"And he said, 'Morning or afternoon?' And the bureaucrat said, 'Well, wait a minute, we're talking about ten years from now. What difference does it make?'

" 'The plumber is coming in the morning,' said the young man."

In much the same vein, Reagan described two Soviet citizens who were debating the difference between their country's constitution and its American counterpart.

"That's easy," said one. "The Soviet Constitution guarantees freedom of speech and freedom of gathering. The American Constitution guarantees freedom after speech and freedom after gathering."

In Reagan's book, a Communist is someone who reads Marx and Lenin. A noncommunist is someone who understands Marx and Lenin.

"What are the four things wrong with Soviet agriculture?" Reagan asked. "Spring, summer, winter, and fall."

"A star Soviet athlete–a hammer thrower–went to the West, saw what it was really like, and then returned home. And in the first meet after he got back, he set a new world record. A journalist from a Soviet newspaper rushed up to him and asked, 'Comrade, how did you manage to throw your hammer that far?' And he replied, 'Give me a sickle, and I'll throw it even farther.'"

Reagan was also fond of a double-edged Irish blessing: "May those who love us, love us. And those who don't love us, may God turn their hearts. And if He doesn't turn their hearts, may He turn their ankles, so we'll know them by their limping."

Reagan was once asked why he was addressing a Future Farmers of America gathering, in Las Vegas of all places. "Buster," he replied, "they're in a business that makes a Las Vegas crap table look like a guaranteed annual income."

Reagan identified a voter who, when asked whether the biggest problem confronting the nation was ignorance or apathy, replied, "I don't know, and I don't care."

Reagan poor-mouthed his fund-raising abilities. In fact, he went on, "That's why I got into government, because we don't ask for it, we just take it."

Before another gathering of reporters, Reagan tweaked the fourth estate. "I thought it was extraordinary that Richard Nixon went on *Meet the Press* and spent an entire hour with Chris Wallace, Tom Brokaw, and John Chancellor. That should put an end to the talk that he hasn't been punished enough."

Reagan didn't need speechwriters; he had a natural flair for one-liners. For example, there was his definition of *status quo*–"Latin for the mess we're in." Then there was the day he met South Africa's Bishop Desmond Tutu in the Oval Office. Afterward someone asked, "What did you think of Tutu?"

"So-so," said Reagan.

Reagan was a master at self-deprecation, especially on the subject of his age. "When I was in fifth grade," he once said, "I'm not sure that I knew what a national debt was. Of course, when I was in the fifth grade, we didn't have one."

Before a church audience, the president recalled the shortest sermon he'd ever heard, delivered one sweltering Sunday morning in his hometown of Dixon, Illinois. Declared the preacher, "If you think it's hot today, just wait."

Once, called upon to introduce Bob Hope at a banquet, the president identified Hope's two great loves. "He loves to entertain the troops and he loves golf. Just the other day he asked me, 'What's your handicap?' and I said, 'Congress.'"

#3 Franklin D. Roosevelt

As a Harvard undergraduate, FDR foreshadowed his New Deal programs by enrolling in the Harvard Social Service Society, doing missionary work, and attending a course taught by Professor Francis Peabody, "Ethics of the Social Questions"–popularly known around campus as "Peabo's Drainage, Drunkenness, and Divorces."

Reporters found it impossible to dislike a president who abandoned the formal tradition of submitting written questions, and who often behaved as one of the boys. For his part, Roosevelt chuckled over parodies of his alphabet-soup agencies, including this anthem penned by the *Chicago Tribune*'s Walter Trohan:

> My country 'tis of thee
> Sweet land of liberty
> FDIC.
> AAA, NRA,
> CCC, RFC,
> PWA, WPA,
> HOLC.

Roosevelt exchanged bantering messages with reporters, even at public events. Once Trohan accompanied the president on a visit to Harvard. The occasion–the induction of Franklin Jr. into the august Fly Club. Impishly the *Tribune* correspondent sent a note to the president informing him that he, Trohan, had attended Notre Dame, as a consequence of which he might have joined the Knights of Columbus. Thus he was all the more impressed by such distinguished clubmen as the Roosevelts.

Back came the reply in FDR's scrawl: "Shoo, fly, don't bother me."

FDR gave perhaps the best speechmaking advice ever recorded when he said, "Be sincere; be brief; be seated."

From his first day in office, Roosevelt experimented with new ideas. Consistency was not his hobgoblin. At the same time, he wasn't afraid to make mistakes. "I have no expectation of making a hit every time I come to bat," he explained to an aide. "What I seek is the highest possible batting average."

In 1934, FDR dismayed reformers by naming the financier Joseph P. Kennedy to be chairman of the new Securities and Exchange Commission. Even Democratic National Chairman Jim Farley protested the appointment, reminding Roosevelt of the sometimes unscrupulous methods employed in building the Kennedy fortune.

FDR was unfazed and unpersuaded. He had his own rationale for putting Kennedy in charge of Wall Street. As he put it, "Set a thief to catch a thief."

Although America's newspaper publishers generally opposed his policies, FDR usually managed to get the last word. He was especially cutting in his remarks about the prominent columnist Walter Lippmann, "whose English is so limpid and so pure that the trigonometry of public affairs is made clear overnight to the kindergartens of America."

Alice Roosevelt Longworth was no fan of "the Hyde Park Roosevelts." Of her distinguished kinsman Franklin, she pronounced him "two-thirds mush and one-third Eleanor."

In the 1936 election, Roosevelt had a field day with so-called "me too" Republicans. Addressing a Democratic audience in New York that September, the president was at the top of his form. "Let me warn the nation against the smooth evasion which says, 'Of course we believe all these things; we believe in Social Security; we believe in work for the unemployed; we believe in saving homes. Cross our hearts and hope to die, we believe in all these things; but we do not like the way the present administration is doing them. Just turn them over to us. We will do all of them—we will do more of them—we will do them better; and, most important of all, the doing of them will not cost anybody anything.'"

Then as now, economics was the dismal science. Roosevelt said as much in writing to the noted Harvard professor Joseph Schumpeter in December 1936. "Thirty-six years ago, I began a more or less intensive study of economics and economists," said the president. "The course has continued with growing intensity, especially during the last four years. As a result, I am compelled to admit—or boast—whichever way you care to put it—that I know nothing of economics and that nobody else does either!"

In speaking to the Daughters of the American Revolution, Roosevelt could not resist a none too subtle dig at the organization's pretensions. He began by addressing them as "fellow immigrants," then added that "through no fault of my own . . . I am descended from a number of people who came over on the

Mayflower. More than that, every one of my ancestors on both sides—and when you go back four generations or five generations, it means thirty-two or sixty-four of them—every single one of them, without exception, was in this land in 1776. And there was only one Tory among them.

"The text is this: remember, remember always that all of us, and you and I especially, are descended from immigrants and revolutionists."

Roosevelt enjoyed twitting his political enemies, especially those who portrayed him as a clear and present danger to American institutions. Thus he began an address at the University of North Carolina in December 1938 as follows:

> You undergraduates who see me for the first time have read in your newspapers and heard on the air that I am, at the very least, an ogre—a consorter with Communists, a destroyer of the rich, a breaker of our ancient traditions. Some of you think of me perhaps as the inventor of the economic royalist, of the wicked utilities, of the money changers of the Temple. You have heard for six years that I was about to plunge the nation into war; that you and your little brothers would be sent to the bloody fields of battle in Europe; that I was driving the nation into bankruptcy; and that I breakfasted every morning on a dish of "grilled millionaire."
>
> Actually, I am an exceedingly mild-mannered person—a practitioner of peace, both domestic and foreign, a believer in the capitalistic system, and for my breakfast a devotee of scrambled eggs.

FDR's first secretary of the navy, Claude Swanson, was a former Democratic senator from Virginia of middling talents and flexible principles. After suddenly switching his position on a controversial issue, Swanson explained himself in words that have echoed through many a congressional and White House chamber. According to Swanson, "My constituents can't change their minds any faster than I can."

Eleanor Roosevelt was dubbed "Our Flying First Lady" by *Good Housekeeping* magazine. Leaving the White House one morning to visit a penitentiary in Baltimore, she was careful not to disturb FDR. When he subsequently asked Mrs. Roosevelt's secretary about his wife's absence, he was told, "She's in prison, Mr. President."

"I'm not surprised," responded FDR, "but what for?"

Washington is a town where ambition is exceeded only by ingratitude. As evidence of this, FDR's secretary once inquired whether the president had heard of an old friend who was being very critical of him. "That's strange," said Roosevelt, "I don't recall ever doing him any favors."

Roosevelt was a master at coddling difficult colleagues. Harold Ickes, his temperamental secretary of the interior, was widely criticized for fuel shortages on the East Coast during the winter of 1941. FDR took it upon himself to mollify the prickly secretary with a presidential limerick:

> There was a lady of fashion,
> Who had a terrific passion.
> As she jumped into bed,
> She casually said,
> "Here's one thing that Ickes can't ration."

For years Roosevelt and his supporters personalized the Great Depression as Herbert Hoover's doing. Not even the advent of World War II eased the hard feelings between the two men. Shortly after Pearl Harbor, Roosevelt summoned Bernard Baruch for a discussion of manpower shortages and how best to streamline a chaotic home front. Baruch urged him to send for Hoover. What's more, said Baruch, he had reason to believe that the former president would gladly contribute his services for the war's duration.

Roosevelt would have none of it. "I'm not Jesus Christ," he snapped, "and I'm not going to raise him from the dead."

At a presidential press conference in April 1941, a reporter asked if Roosevelt's friend Harry Hopkins would be serving the government as a "dollar-a-year man."

The president: "No, he will not."

Question: "Will he be an administrative assistant, then, sir?"

The president: "No, I don't know what he will be, but he won't be a dollar-a-year man."

Question: "Will he get paid?"

The president: "Yes, sure, he's a Democrat! What a foolish question."

Roosevelt enlivened a White House gathering in 1943 by recalling the first order he had issued following a White House meeting on Pearl Harbor. Summoning the chief of army engineers, he had banned the construction of any temporary buildings in the nation's capital without presidential authorization. An angry general demanded justification for such an edict, which went against precedents established in World War I.

Exactly, replied Roosevelt, who pointed with his cigarette holder in the general direction of Washington's Mall. "General, you just go to that window and tell me whether the Navy and Munitions Buildings are still there."

They were, nearly a quarter century after their construction.

The general said as much. "That's just what I mean, General," said FDR. "*Not temporary.* Now you go right back to your office and design me some really temporary buildings, guaranteed to fall down within seven years; for this war can't possibly last that long. And I'll initial any plans you bring me with great pleasure. But remember, seven years!"

In his 1944 campaign against Tom Dewey, FDR achieved political immortality with the ultimate shaggy-dog story. Before a union audience in Washington, D.C., the president mocked Republican leaders, "not content with attacks on me, or my wife, or on my sons. No, not content with that, they now include my little dog, Fala. Well, of course, I don't resent attacks, and my family doesn't resent attacks, but Fala does resent them. You know, Fala is Scotch, and being a Scotty, as soon as he learned that the Republican fiction writers in Congress and out had concocted a story that I had left him behind on the Aleutian Islands and had sent a destroyer back to find him—at a cost to the taxpayers of two or three, or eight or twenty million dollars—his Scotch soul was furious. He has not been the same dog since. I am accustomed to hearing malicious falsehoods about myself—such as that old, worm-eaten chestnut that I have represented myself as indispensable. But I think I have a right to resent, to object to libelous statements about my dog."

Thereafter wags said it was a campaign between Roosevelt's dog and Dewey's goat.

FDR was a master storyteller who often employed his talents to divert attention from potentially unpleasant subjects. The first time a young congressman named Lyndon Johnson arranged an

Oval Office meeting with the president, it was in hopes of obtaining Rural Electrification Administration funding for Johnson's impoverished Texas district. As it happened, he barely got a word in edgewise as FDR discussed everything from the design of multiarch dams to the physique of Russian women.

The next time, LBJ came prepared—complete with charts, maps, and plentiful statistics. Even before Roosevelt opened his mouth, Johnson made his pitch: "Water, water everywhere and not a drop to drink; public power everywhere and not a drop for my poor people." For the next ten minutes, Johnson monopolized the conversation. The minifilibuster proved successful. He got the REA funding. What's more, he made a permanent impression on FDR, who knew a master talker when he heard one.

Roosevelt loved to tell the story of the Wall Street executive who would buy a newspaper each morning, look at the front page, swear, and throw the unread paper in the trash can. One day, the newspaper-stand operator asked the executive what he was doing day after day.

"I'm looking for an obituary," said the businessman.

"But, sir, obituaries aren't on the front page—they are toward the back."

"Son," said the executive, "you better believe that the obituary I'm looking for will be on the front page."

#4 THEODORE ROOSEVELT

There had never been a president like Theodore Roosevelt. In the words of his admirer William Allen White, "The gift of the gods to Theodore Roosevelt was joy, joy in life. He took joy in everything he did, in hunting, camping, and ranching, in politics, in reforming the police of the civil service, in organizing and commanding the Rough Riders." And then White admitted, "Roosevelt bit me and I went mad."

"Perhaps others have lived longer in the place and enjoyed it quite as much," said TR on the eve of his departure from Washington, "but none have ever really had more fun out of it than we have." Rooseveltian fun included daughter Alice, wreathed in cigarette smoke and with her pet snake Emily Spinach wrapped around her neck, hiding beneath the main staircase of the White House. Princess Alice liked nothing better than to jump out and tell unsuspecting tourists that the president of the United States beat his children every day.

Thus it came as no surprise when TR announced, "I can be president of the United States, or I can govern Alice, but I cannot possibly do both." According to the first lady, she had *six* children, "of whom Theodore is the youngest." When not engaged in jujitsu matches in the East Room or pillow fights with his children, the president led a chase for rats in the State Dining Room. "This house is rotten with dogs," declared his wife. Horses, too—among them a pony named General Grant, and Algonquin, a calico creature that rode a White House elevator one day to the second-floor sickroom of little Archie Roosevelt.

"A nervous person had no business around the White House in those days," according to chief usher Ike Hoover. "He was sure to be a wreck in a very short time."

It was said after TR's first formal address to Congress that the Government Printing Office had exhausted its supply of the personal pronoun. The famous humorist Mr. Dooley read Roosevelt's *The Rough Riders*, a swashbuckling account of his part in the Spanish-American War, and suggested that the book be retitled *Alone in Cuba*.

In another column, Mr. Dooley described the apostle of the strenuous life as he vacationed at Oyster Bay: "4 A.M., horseback ride, the president instructing his two sons, age two and four respectively, to jump the First Methodist Church without knocking off the shingles; 6 A.M., wrestles with trained grizzly bear; 7 A.M., breakfast; 8 A.M., Indian clubs; 9 A.M., boxes with Sharkey; 10 A.M., beats the tennis champion; 11 A.M., receives a band of Rough Riders . . . noon, dinner with Sharkey [and a wildly variegated group of guests, whose conversation] dealt with art, boxing, literature, horse breaking, science, shooting, politics, how to kill a mountain lion, diplomacy, lobbying, poetry, the pivot blow, reform, and the campaign in Cuba."

Delighting in his unofficial role as national adviser at large on things in general, the president preached the virtues of phonetic spelling, called playwright George Bernard Shaw a "blue-rumped ape" and Thomas Paine "a filthy little atheist." TR's critics were flailed as "copper-riveted idiots" and "circumcised skunks."

Having invented the bully pulpit, Roosevelt used it to enlist public support for the Panama Canal and Western conservation. Yet another crusade, against what Roosevelt called "embalmed beef," was inspired by muckraking journalists, who exposed sickening conditions in the meatpacking industry. In the words of the *New York Evening Post:*

> Mary had a little lamb
> And when she saw it sicken
> She shipped it off to Packing Town
> And now it's labeled chicken.

Reporters were drawn to the Roosevelt White House like filings to a magnet. One magazine of the era captured the president's exuberant news value by headlining a profile, "The Scrapes He Gets Into, The Scrapes He Gets Out Of; The Things He Attempts, the Things He Accomplishes; His Appointments and His Disappointments; The Rebukes That He Administers and Those He Receives; His Assumptions, Presumptions, Omnitions and Deficiencies, Make Up a Daily Tale Which Those of Us Who Survived His Tenure of the President's Office Will Doubtless Miss, As We Might Miss Some Property of the Atmosphere We Breathe."

During the 1902 coal strike, Roosevelt's good friend Henry Cabot Lodge despaired of the political consequences of inaction. "Isn't there something we can appear to be doing?" he remarked to the president. TR had already worked himself into a lather over mounting coal shortages. Summoning a friendly senator to the White House, he gave vent to his frustration.

"I am the president of the United States, I am the commander in chief of the army. I will see that the people have coal!"

"But, Mr. President," said the lawmaker, "what do you expect to do with the Constitution of the United States, which provides for property rights and regards them as sacred?"

Roosevelt's face grew red, and his voice rose to falsetto pitch. "To hell with the Constitution when the people want coal!" His guest then hurried to the home of "Uncle Joe" Cannon, a powerful Republican in the House.

The president couldn't possibly have said such a thing, Cannon told his informant.

"Go ask him about it yourself, if you don't believe me," said the senator.

An hour later, Uncle Joe returned with a look of amazement on his face and said, "That fellow in the White House did say that. I went over and talked to him about it myself, and he said exactly that same thing to me, and, by God, I'm afraid of him!"

When Theodore Roosevelt refurbished the White House in 1902, he discarded his predecessor's potted palms, not to mention the ornate Tiffany screens installed by President Arthur. Mooseheads took up residence in the State Dining Room. Among the more valuable trappings sold at auction was a beautiful old sideboard, once presented to Lemonade Lucy Hayes by the Women's Christian Temperance Union. Ironically, this monument to sobriety was sold to a saloonkeeper on Pennsylvania Avenue, prompting bitter attacks on Roosevelt by publicity-seeking congressmen.

Uncle Joe Cannon took the floor in TR's defense. "Tradition tells us that on rainy days Dolley Madison used to hang the White House washing on an old-fashioned clothesline in the East Room," said Cannon. "My God, where is that clothesline?"

TR's revolutionary plan to dig an isthmian canal in the newly declared Republic of Panama was the subject of considerable jest.

"Have they decided whether it will be lock or sea level?" ran one inquiry.

"It is going to be unlock."

"Unlock what?"

"Unlock the Treasury."

In criticizing "malefactors of great wealth," Roosevelt did not spare members of the educated class. "A man who has never gone to school may steal from a freight car," he once gibed, "but if he has a university education, he may steal the whole railroad."

A visiting British politician fell under the president's spell. As he put it, "The two things in America which seem to me extraordinary are Niagara Falls and President Roosevelt."

Not everyone was impressed by Roosevelt. The muckraking journalist Lincoln Steffens regarded the president as an opportunist, more picturesque than profound. At a meeting one day staffers told TR that he didn't stand for anything fundamental. "All you represent is the square deal."

"That's it!" Roosevelt shouted. "That's my slogan." He pounded the desk for emphasis. "The square deal. I'll throw that out in my next statement." And so was born one of the most potent slogans in American history.

Even the sourpuss Henry Adams contracted Roosevelt fever. "That he is still a bore as big as a buffalo I do not deny," wrote Adams, "but at least he is a different sort." Of all the presidents that ever lived, Adams went on, "Theodore thinks of nothing, talks of nothing, and lives for nothing but his political interest. If you remark to him that God is Great, he asks naively at once how that will affect his election."

Mark Twain, on the other hand, declared TR "the most formidable disaster that has befallen the country since the Civil War." By 1907 the famed author resorted to one of his own creations to describe the egocentric president. "Mr. Roosevelt," wrote Twain, "is the Tom Sawyer of the political world . . . always showing off; always hunting a chance to show off; in his frenzied imagination, the Great Republic is a vast Barnum circus with him for a clown and the whole world for an audience; he would go to Halifax for half a chance to show off; and he would go to hell for a whole one."

The acerbic Speaker Tom Reed mocked the inventor of the bully pulpit. "Theodore," said Reed, "if there is one thing more than another for which I admire you, it is your original discovery of the Ten Commandments."

TR's letters to his children comprise some of the most delightful accounts of life in the White House. In March 1904 the president briefed his son Kermit on his latest athletic enthusiasm: "I'm wrestling with two Japanese wrestlers three times a week. I am not the age or the build one would think to be whirled lightly over an opponent's head and batted down to the mattress without damage. But they're so skillful that I have not been hurt at all. My throat is a little sore, because once when one of them had me in a stranglehold, I also got hold of his windpipe and thought I could perhaps choke him off before he could choke me. However, he got ahead."

TR was just as amusing in recounting his journey down the Mississippi Valley in the fall of 1907. "The first part of my trip . . . was just about in the ordinary style. I had continually to rush out to wave at the people in the towns through which the train passed. If the train stopped anywhere, I had to make a very short speech to several hundred people who evidently thought they liked me, and whom I really liked, but to whom I had nothing in the world to say. . . . When I got on the boat, however, times grew easier. I still had to rush out continually, stand in the front part of the deck, and wave at groups of people onshore, and at stem-wheel steamboats draped with American flags and loaded with enthusiastic excursionists. But I had a great deal of time for myself, and by gentle firmness I think I have succeeded in impressing on my good hosts that I rather resent allopathic doses of information about shoals and dikes, the amount of sand per cubic foot of water, the quantity of manufacture supplied by each river town, etc."

Besides the horses, dogs, and hens named Fierce and Baron Speckle, the Roosevelt White House featured "the cunningest kitten I have ever seen," a prankish creature known as Tom Quartz. TR captured the scene as Tom made the acquaintance of Speaker of the House Joseph Cannon, "an exceedingly solemn, elderly gentleman with chin whiskers, who certainly does not look to be of playful nature."

"He is a great friend of mine," TR reported to his son Kermit, "and we sat talking over what our policies for this session should be until about eleven o'clock; and when he went away, I accompanied him to the head of the stairs. He had gone about halfway down when Tom Quartz strolled by, his tail erect and very fluffy. He spied Mr. Cannon going down the stairs, jumped to the conclusion that he was a playmate escaping, and raced after him, suddenly grasping him by the leg the way he does Archie and Quentin when they play hide-and-seek with him; then loosening his hold he tore downstairs ahead of Mr. Cannon, who eyed him with iron calm and not one particle of surprise."

Sometimes TR was too candid for his own good. For example, there was his definition of "the most successful politician" as "he who says what everybody is thinking and in the loudest voice."

A proponent of political reform and leadership by what he called the governing class, the idealistic Roosevelt said that "no people is wholly civilized where the distinction is drawn between stealing an office and stealing a purse."

Himself a graduate of Harvard, Roosevelt wasn't particularly impressed by educational pedigree. "A muttonhead, after an education at West Point—or Harvard—is a muttonhead still," he observed.

Yankee Wits

#5 Calvin Coolidge

The sharp-tongued Alice Roosevelt Longworth declared that Coolidge looked as if he had been weaned on a pickle. To William Allen White, he was "this runty, aloof, little man who quacks through his nose when he speaks."

Coolidge found his future wife, Miss Grace Goodhue, in Northampton, Massachusetts, where she was employed as a teacher at the Clark School for the Deaf. Grace's subsequent marriage to the man popularly known as Silent Cal led at least one wag to say of her that "having taught the deaf to hear, she might yet cause the dumb to speak."

Returning early from their honeymoon in Montreal, Grace quickly found herself saddled with no fewer than fifty-seven pairs of stockings, all requiring darning. The bride asked her husband whether he had married her for her knitting skills. "No," replied Coolidge, "but I find them mighty handy."

The Coolidges for many years lived in a small duplex in Northampton, whose monthly rent did not exceed $28. Over the mantelpiece in the living room was an embroidered quotation, which might have summed up Coolidge's public persona:

> A wise old owl sat on an oak,
> The more he saw, the less he spoke;
> The less he spoke, the more he heard,
> Why can't we be like that old bird?

Grace told of a visiting Baptist preacher entertained as a dinner guest at the Coolidge home. As it happened, the minister ate little, explaining that he never took much nourishment before addressing a revival meeting. Later that evening, her husband returned from the meeting. Grace asked for an assessment of their guest's performance.

"Might as well have et," said Coolidge.

Thrifty as ever, Coolidge lamented that "nothing is easier than spending the public money. It does not appear to belong to anybody."

Coolidge's sole electoral defeat came at the hand of one John J. Kennedy, a Northampton insurance man who nosed out his Republican opponent in a 1905 race for that city's school committee. As luck would have it, the election took place a few weeks after Coolidge and his bride returned from their Montreal honeymoon. So when he heard a neighbor justify his vote for Kennedy on the grounds that committee members should have children of their own in the public schools, Coolidge had a terse rejoinder.

"Might give me time," he said.

As state-senate president in Massachusetts, Coolidge used humor to defuse a potentially nasty confrontation. When a colleague complained that he had been told by another member in debate to go to hell, Coolidge interrupted. "I've examined the constitution and the senate rules," he drawled, "and there's nothing in them that compels you to go."

Coolidge earned his reputation as a man of few words. "If you don't say anything," he once remarked, "you won't be called on to repeat it." Hoping to fill a long silence with small talk, one visitor looked out the window one soggy afternoon and noted, "I wonder if it will ever stop raining."

"Well," replied Coolidge, "it always has."

When Coolidge was unexpectedly nominated for vice president in 1920, a reporter from Massachusetts who knew him offered to bet his colleagues a dinner that Warren Harding would die in office, thereby enabling the famously lucky Coolidge to succeed to the nation's highest office. Others were even more contemptuous of the closemouthed Yankee. In the words of one Democratic observer, Coolidge was "distinguishable from the furniture only when he moved."

Will Rogers had a field day with Coolidge's breakfast meetings for Capitol Hill lawmakers, at which food and conversation alike were rationed. Truth be told, the president seemed more comfortable around animals than people. Frequently he looked the other way as his collies helped themselves to morning sausages, and licked the sugar out of the bottom of his empty coffee cup.

According to Rogers, the dogs were treated so much better than the human guests, he seriously considered getting down on all fours and crawling up to the president's side to get enough to eat.

Rogers wasn't exaggerating when he said that Coolidge wasted more humor on the uncomprehending than any other man in public life. On encountering the president outside the White House, Rogers asked tongue in cheek, "What sort of crooks and horse thieves did you meet today, Mr. President?"

"The cabinet," said Coolidge.

Press criticism rolled off Coolidge's back. When an agitated Herbert Hoover protested an unfriendly column in the *American Mercury,* Coolidge was unimpressed. "You mean that one in the magazine with the green cover?" he asked Hoover. "I started to read it, but it was against me, so I didn't finish it."

One of Coolidge's first orders on becoming president was to tell chief usher Ike Hoover, "I want things as they used to be—before." The rebuke to his boozy predecessor was implied, but unmistakable. According to Alice Roosevelt Longworth, the atmosphere of the post-Harding White House "was as different as a New England front parlor is from a back room in a speakeasy."

Urged to increase spending on military aviation, Coolidge asked his cabinet, "Why can't we just buy one airplane and have all the pilots take turns?"

To a senator who had just returned from Minnesota, Coolidge directed the requisite inquiries about the Midwestern weather. When his guest reciprocated, the president said with his best deadpan expression, "Well, it's been hot here. I was sitting here the other night with a lady who fainted. Don't know whether it was the weather or the conversation."

Unbought and unbossed, to use a Yankee phrase, Coolidge was as independent as a hog on ice. Once a friend presented him a copy of the *Intimate Papers of Colonel House,* documenting the activities of Wilson's alter ego. Coolidge took the opportunity to upbraid his own would-be sponsor, Frank Stearns, a Boston merchant popularly known as Lord Lingerie. "An unofficial adviser to a president of the United States is not a good thing," Coolidge told Stearns.

"Did I ever try to advise you?" Stearns asked.

"No," replied Coolidge, "but I thought I'd better tell you."

Calvin Coolidge didn't say very much, according to Will Rogers, and even when he did, he didn't say very much. Justice Holmes had his own explanation for the president's success in a nation weary of wartime sacrifice and postwar scandal. "While I don't expect anything astonishing from [Coolidge]," said Holmes, "I don't want anything astonishing."

The Coolidge White House boasted a small menagerie of pets, most sent as gifts by admirers. There were a pair of lion cubs, named Tax Resolution and Budget Bureau; a black bear from Mexico; an Australian wallaby; a cat dubbed Mud, "for anyone can see that his name is mud," explained the president; and

Rebecca the raccoon, a particular favorite that was draped about the presidential neck as Coolidge strode up and down White House corridors. Originally intended to be part of the family's Thanksgiving dinner, Rebecca quickly earned a place in Coolidge's heart; the pet proved quite the gourmet herself, dining on green shrimp, chicken, persimmon, and eggs.

The most famous Coolidge pets were the collies Prudence Prim and Rob Roy. The latter posed alongside the first lady for her official portrait by Howard Chandler Christy. To establish a contrast with the animal's white coat, Mrs. Coolidge was urged to don a red dress.

"Why don't you keep your white dress on," cracked the president, "and dye the dog red."

One of the most democratic of America's presidents, Coolidge made little effort to conceal his distaste for snobs. Once he was accosted at a White House reception by a large, self-satisfied matron whose accent identified her Beacon Hill origins.

"I come from Boston," she announced.

"Yes," said Coolidge, "and you'll never get over it."

In modern terms, Coolidge was a control freak. He prohibited his wife from driving, horseback riding, flying in an airplane, bobbing her hair, or wearing slacks. He chose her hats. Finally, one morning over breakfast, Grace rebelled. She knew nothing of her engagements, she complained. Couldn't the Secret Service prepare each day a list of the coming week's programs? she asked.

Coolidge peered over the top of his newspaper. "Grace," he remarked, "we don't give out that information promiscuously."

As president, Coolidge supervised White House provisions from the nearest Piggly Wiggly store. He was especially upset by food mysteriously vanishing from White House kitchens. "Too many stews," he once complained. "But then I suppose you can't put a stew in your pocket and carry it home like a pork chop."

Throughout the Coolidge presidency, the White House featured a daily reception for members of the public who wished to shake the president's hand. Coolidge once set a record of 2,096 people in a little over an hour. He rather enjoyed the ritual—what William Howard Taft disparaged as "pump-handle work." Coolidge was less tolerant of formal receptions, since these were customarily filled to overflowing with the verbose and self-important. According to Coolidge's Secret Service agent, "Whenever he spotted a particularly bejeweled dowager down the line, or a social leader of rank and distinction, he would nudge me and say, 'Colonel, stop the line at that lady there. I've got to rest.' And then, while the lady waited, he would go and sit down for five or ten minutes."

H. L. Mencken set the tone for later historians when he said that Coolidge's ideal day "is one in which nothing would ever happen."

One day in December 1924, a newsreel man shouted at the president, "Look pleasant and for heaven's sake say something—anything; good morning or howdy do!"

Coolidge turned to his companion and said, "That man gets more conversation out of me than all Congress."

Coolidge enjoyed putting down sycophants. One overeager admirer rushed up to him and gushed, "Mr. President, I was so anxious to hear your speech at the opening of Congress, I had to stand the *whole* forty-five minutes."

"So did I," said Coolidge.

When a congressman asked for the newest presidential photograph, Coolidge replied, "I don't know what you want another for. I'm using the same face."

Coolidge was characteristically modest about his speechwriting abilities. "I always knew that there was some water in my well, but that I had to pump to get it. It is not a gushing fountain."

One of the major embarrassments of the Coolidge administration occurred when Vice President Charles Dawes slept through the Senate confirmation vote for attorney general in 1925. As a result, a major presidential nominee went down to defeat for the first time in sixty years. An enterprising wag put up a sign outside the vice president's hotel, proclaiming DAWES SLEPT HERE. Amidst all the laughter at his expense, Dawes found one true friend in Chief Justice William Howard Taft, whose public naps were the stuff of legend. Visiting the Supreme Court one day, the vice president couldn't help but notice that Taft himself was yawning on the bench. On spotting Dawes, Taft promptly sent down a note to him: "Come up here, this is a good place to sleep."

It's not hard to see where Coolidge came by his distrust of the rest of the world. Once he asked how a friend's daughter was doing in school. As it happened, the young woman had just brought home her first French book to show her parents.

"Does she know all the English ones?" asked Coolidge.

There was more to Coolidge's thrift than cheeseparing. "I favor the policy of economy," he once said, "not because I wish to save money, but because I wish to save people."

When asked how he got his exercise, the president slyly answered, "Having my picture taken." In fact, at various times Coolidge let photographers depict him wearing cowboy chaps, a Boy Scout getup, farming overalls, and full Sioux Indian regalia. "Oh, Mammy," he told his wife, "they're making a perfect fool out of me." On second thought, he concluded that presidential dignity could be overrated. After all, said the dour Yankee, "It's good for people to laugh."

Traditionalist though he might have been in his politics, Coolidge was not above defacing White House portraits. One evening, clearly distracted by something outside the State Dining Room, he turned to his secretary of commerce: "Mr. Hoover, don't you think the light has been a little too shiny on Mr. John Quincy Adams's head?" Without pausing for reply, Coolidge summoned a servant and stepladder, rubbed a rag in some fireplace ashes, and then blacked out the bald, ample cranium of the sixth president.

Only later did it fall to Hoover to apologize to his own secretary of the navy, Charles Francis Adams, for the disfigurement of his ancestor. One way or another, Hoover seemed fated to suffer from his predecessor's conduct.

At the summer White House in South Dakota, Coolidge wore white gloves when fishing, at least until his wife's ridicule drove him to exchange them for a darker shade. Secret Service men baited the presidential fishhook and retrieved his catch. They also seized trout taken by an itinerant sportsman bold enough to test the waters fully two miles away from the executive retreat. "They are *my* fish," said Coolidge.

When a luncheon guest refused a postmeal cigar, explaining that he was unable to hold one in his false teeth, Coolidge proposed a wicked solution: Why not have a little wire platform made to attach to his chin to rest the cigar on?

A practical joker, Coolidge bestowed nicknames on White House staffers. A veteran doorman became "The Mink," while butler Thomas Rouch was christened "Bug." The Coolidges entertained former secretary of state Charles Evans Hughes—the same dignified jurist whom TR had ridiculed as "a bearded icicle." Each morning, the presidential barber, clad in white, starched coat and carrying a towel draped over his arm, appeared outside Coolidge's bedroom.

"I do not want any haircut or shave," said Coolidge, "but I want you to go up . . . to the bedroom which is being occupied by Justice Hughes. Knock on the door and ask him if he doesn't want a shave."

He didn't.

At other times, Coolidge liked nothing better than to ring all the bells on his desk, or press a buzzer alerting doormen, ushers, elevator operators, and policemen of his impending arrival—while he disappeared out a side entrance of the White House to go window-shopping.

Not long before he left the White House, Coolidge declared, "Perhaps one of the most important accomplishments of my administration has been minding my own business."

Having established a reputation for verbal as well as fiscal thrift, Coolidge made it work for him. "I always figured the American public wanted a solemn ass for president," he remarked in a candid moment, "so I went along with them." More typical was Coolidge's observation "I have noticed that nothing I never said ever did me any harm."

Coolidge enjoyed pulling journalists' legs. At a White House press conference a reporter asked him, "Do you have any comments about tariffs, Mr. President?"
   "No," said Coolidge.
   "Do you have any comment about the farm bill?"
   "No."
   "Do you have any comment about the naval appropriation?"
   "No."
   As the newsmen were filing out of the Oval Office, they heard Coolidge cackle, "And don't quote me!"

Not long before leaving office, Coolidge made a bitter prophecy to an associate. "Well," he observed, "they're going to elect that superman Hoover, and he's going to have some trouble. He's going to have to spend money. But he won't spend enough. Then the Democrats will come in and spend money like water. But they don't know anything about money. Then they will want me to come back and save some money for them. But I won't do it."

"You have to stand every day three or four hours of visitors," Coolidge warned his successor shortly before handing power over to Herbert Hoover. "Nine-tenths of them want something they ought not to have. If you keep dead still, they will run down in three or four minutes. If you even cough or smile, they will start up all over again."

Not long after leaving the White House, Coolidge traveled to Florida to dedicate the Singing Tower, erected by philanthropist Edward Bok. Asked to describe the monument, Coolidge replied, "Bok is dedicating it as a bird sanctuary, and putting up these bells to interest the birds in music."

Returning in 1929 to his old duplex in Northampton, Coolidge found he could no longer walk on his front porch or stroll unmolested through the streets of his hometown. Tourists clogged the once quiet street on which the Coolidges lived. Many of the visitors barely hid their disappointment at the modest quarters inhabited by the former president. "I don't think much of this place," muttered one out-of-towner in a voice loud enough to be overheard.

"Democrats!" said Coolidge.

"I should like to be known," Coolidge once asserted, "as a former president who tries to mind his own business." Part of that business was a nationally syndicated daily newspaper column. Detractors compared Coolidge's bland messages to advertisements for Wanamaker's Department Store. Will Rogers dissented, sort of. There was nothing wrong, said the comedian, with adopting a spiritual tack to the problems of Depression-era America. Indeed, said Rogers, Coolidge "wants us to get back to the old early New England tradition, where if he wasn't praying, he was burning somebody that was."

Coolidge seemed unruffled by the controversy. "They criticize me for harping on the obvious," he told a friend. "Perhaps someday I'll write one on 'The Importance of the Obvious.' If all the folks in the United States would do the few simple things they know they ought to do, most of our big problems would take care of themselves."

One of Coolidge's most persistent critics was the essayist and professional wit Dorothy Parker. On being informed that the former president was dead in January 1933, the acid-tongued Miss Parker responded, "How could they tell?"

#6 JOHN F. KENNEDY

In 1958, JFK brought laughter—and made political points—in describing a recession. "As I interpret [President Eisenhower], we're now at the end of the beginning of the upturn of the downturn. Every bright spot the White House finds in the economy is like the policeman bending over the body in the alley who says cheerfully, "Two of his wounds are fatal—but the other one's not so bad."

When the religious issue surfaced in the 1960 campaign, Kennedy adroitly turned the tables while sharing a platform with his rival at the annual Al Smith dinner hosted by New York's Cardinal Spellman. According to Kennedy, Vice President Nixon had recently been criticized by the *Wall Street Journal.* "That is like *Osservatore Romano* criticizing the pope." Kennedy also twitted Nixon for his criticism of presidents and ex-presidents who resorted to profanity on the stump. As a matter of fact, Kennedy claimed that a Republican supporter had recently praised the vice president for delivering "a damn fine speech," to which Nixon replied, "I appreciate the compliment, but not the language." Not to be denied, his Republican admirer went on, "Yes, sir, I liked it so much I contributed one thousand dollars to your campaign."

"The hell you say," exclaimed Nixon.

During the 1960 campaign, Kennedy's opponent, Richard Nixon, raised the issue of former president Truman's profanity. According to JFK, this prompted the following message from him to the salty Truman. "Dear Mr. President: I have noted your suggestion as to where those who vote for my opponent shall go. While I understand and sympathize with your deep motivation, I think it's important that our side refrain from raising the religious question."

No primary was more critical in 1960 than West Virginia, and to win it, Kennedy campaigned among coal miners deep underground.

"Is it true you're the son of one of our wealthiest men?" one of the miners asked the candidate. Kennedy acknowledged as much.

"Is it true that you've never wanted for anything and had everything you wanted?" he was asked.

"I guess so."

"Is it true you've never done a day's work with your hands all your life?"

Kennedy gave a hesitant nod.

"Well," said the miner, "let me tell you this. You haven't missed a thing."

The 1960 campaign was notable for Kennedy's skillful defusion of the religious issue. After he was attacked by the Reverend Norman Vincent Peale, JFK contrasted his own party's platform, entitled "The Rights of Man," with its Republican counterpart, of which he said, "I do not know its title, but it has been referred to as 'The Power of Positive Thinking.'"

JFK, like other Democratic presidents, relied upon the veteran Washington insider Clark Clifford for advice and guidance. Following his 1960 election victory, Kennedy said he was surprised that the superlawyer Clark had failed to emulate the example of other Democrats clamoring for office after eight long years in the wilderness. As Kennedy put it, "All he asked in return was that we advertise his law firm on the backs of one-dollar bills."

In October 1961, New York columnist Leonard Lyons wrote to Kennedy, informing him that a Madison Avenue storefront was displaying the autographs of several American presidents, and that JFK's signature was selling for more than Teddy Roosevelt's or U. S. Grant's. The president shouldn't bother to acknowledge his letter, added Lyons, for two reasons:

1. You are too busy.
2. If you sign your name too often, that would depress the autograph market on East Fifty-third Street.

A week later JFK responded: "I appreciate your letter about the market on Kennedy signatures. It is hard to believe that the going price is so high now. In order not to depress the market any further, I will not sign this letter. Best regards."

Not signed.

Kennedy enjoyed the antics of Republican Senate leader Everett McKinley Dirksen, the famed Wizard of Ooze who once dismissed a White House budget proposal as having "all the impact of a snowflake on the bosom of the Potomac." During the 1960 campaign, Dirksen had poked fun at Kennedy's frequent absences from the Senate. "We call his the emptiest saddle on the New Frontier," he quipped. Dirksen took a more generous view of Kennedy's famed rocking chair, which the president used to soothe his injured back. "I like rocking chairs," said Dirksen. "They give you a sense of motion without any danger."

Kennedy was not above parodying the soaring rhetoric of his own inaugural address. Before a fund-raising dinner of loyal Democrats, he announced sententiously: "We observe tonight not a celebration of freedom, but a victory of party, for we have sworn to pay off the same party debt our forebears ran up nearly a year and three months ago. Our deficit will not be paid off in the next one hundred days, nor will it be paid off in the first one thousand days, nor in the life of this administration. Nor, perhaps, even in our lifetime on this planet. But let us begin."

Kennedy was just as ironic in describing his wartime experiences aboard PT 109. Asked by a reporter how he became a war hero, the president replied, "It was absolutely involuntary. They sank my boat."

At a July 1963 press conference, JFK was reminded of his 1960 campaign pledge to get America moving again. "Do you think it is moving?" asked a reporter. "And if so, how and where? The reason I ask you the question, Mr. President, is that the Republican National Committee recently adopted a resolution saying you are pretty much a failure."

"I'm sure it was passed unanimously," replied Kennedy.

We forget it now, but at his earliest White House press conferences, JFK read his answers from index cards. As he grew more comfortable with the format, his natural wit surfaced. A *New York Times* reporter observed that as a senator, Kennedy had been more informal. Why, asked the correspondent, was the new president sticking so closely to prepared answers?

"Because I'm not a textual deviant," said Kennedy.

Soon after naming his brother attorney general, Kennedy showed his usual disarming touch when he commented, "I've been criticized by quite a few people for making my brother Bobby attorney general. They didn't realize that I had a very good reason for that appointment. Bobby wants to practice law, and I thought he ought to get a little experience first."

After a dustup with former president Truman, Kennedy said, "I guess Truman will apologize for calling me an SOB, and I will apologize for being one."

The youngest elected president in U.S. history, JFK was only half joking when he said, "It has recently been observed that whether I serve one or two terms in the presidency, I will find myself at the end of that period at what might be called an awkward age—too old to begin a new career, and too young to write my memoirs."

Like FDR, Kennedy was not above using big business as a foil. On one occasion he joked, "I got a letter, the nicest letter I have gotten, actually, since I have been in the White House, from an official of the Bethlehem Steel Company, saying, 'You are even worse than Harry Truman.'"

At a West Point commencement exercise, JFK went beyond standard congratulations in wishing each cadet the greatest success. "I'm not unmindful of the fact that two graduates of the Academy [Grant and Eisenhower] have reached the White House, and neither was a member of my party," said Kennedy. "Until I'm more certain that this trend will be broken, I wish that all of you may be generals and not commanders in chief."

Kennedy's triumphant visit to Paris, where he and his radiant wife, Jacqueline, were guests of President Charles de Gaulle, was the stuff of legend. One evening the president and his guests attended the Paris Ballet. During intermission the imperious de Gaulle permitted some French photographers to take a photograph or two, before airily dismissing them with a contemptuous gesture.

The next day a reporter asked JFK, "Don't you wish you could control your photographers like that?"

To which Kennedy replied, "You must remember that I wasn't called to office as my country's savior."

They might be philosophical opposites, but President Kennedy and Senator Barry Goldwater were actually good friends. Goldwater, a noted photographer, once snapped a picture of the president, which he asked him to autograph. Back it came, with the following inscription: "For Barry Goldwater, whom I urge to follow the career for which he has shown so much talent–photography. From his friend, John Kennedy."

Long before Reagan told Gorbachev jokes, Nikita Khrushchev was the object of a Kennedy story. It seems the Russian premier himself told about one of his countrymen who began running through the Kremlin shouting, "Khrushchev is a fool. Khrushchev is a fool."

For this offense, the intruder was sentenced to twenty-three years in prison, according to Khrushchev, "three for insulting the Party secretary, and twenty for revealing a state secret."

The Kennedys had a compound in the wealthy community of Palm Beach, Florida, where most of their neighbors were staunch Republicans. Returning from a holiday there, JFK said he had entertained doubts about his popularity. "Like members of Congress, I have been, during the last few days over the Easter holiday, back in touch with my constituents and seeing how they felt.

And frankly, I've come back to Washington from Palm Beach and I'm against my entire program."

Ironically for a man attacked because of his faith, as president Kennedy suffered criticism from Catholic Church officials on account of his opposition to federal aid to parochial schools. Having sent his education bill to Congress, the president recalled Al Smith's defeat back in 1928, after which the Democratic candidate had sent a mythical one-word telegram to the pope, reading simply, "Unpack."

After his latest press conference on the school bill, said Kennedy, "I received a one-word wire from the pope: 'Pack.'"

Early in his term, Kennedy was asked by a reporter, "If you had to do it over again, would you work for the presidency and would you recommend the job to others?"

"Well," replied JFK, "the answer to the first is yes, and the answer to the second is no. I don't recommend it to others, at least not for a while."

Plain Speaker, Tall Tales,
and a Poker Face

#7 HARRY TRUMAN

As Truman told it, he had poor vision as a boy and couldn't see well enough to play baseball. "Since I couldn't see the ball, they gave me a special job."

"What was that, Mr. President?" someone asked. "Cheerleader?"

"No," said Truman. "Umpire!"

"I have found the best way to give advice to your children," said Truman, "is to find out what they want and then advise them to do it."

Truman had his own definition of executive responsibility, one rarely taught by political scientists: "The president spends most of his time kissing people on the cheek in order to get them to do what they ought to do without getting kissed."

After World War II, Republican Senator Arthur Vandenberg of Michigan became synonymous with bipartisan foreign policy. Vandenberg proved critical to the passage of such Truman initiatives as NATO and the Marshall Plan. In return, Vandenberg asked only one thing from the president. "If you want us there for the landing, be sure to include us in the takeoff." Truman followed this advice, with historic consequences in the Cold War.

It was no secret that Truman didn't exactly see eye to eye with Colonel Robert R. McCormick, the rabidly partisan publisher of the *Chicago Tribune*. It was McCormick's custom to collect pieces of historic structures for insertion in the outer walls of the fortresslike Tribune Tower. When halfway through his second term Truman undertook the renovation of the White House, the Colonel ordered his Washington bureau chief to obtain a piece of the old structure. Henceforth, McCormick informed his representative, the stone was keeping better company than in its original home.

Notwithstanding his tongue-lashing of the so-called Do Nothing Eightieth Congress, Truman compiled a historic legislative record, especially in the field of bipartisan foreign policy. This didn't keep him from complaining about lawmakers. "If you tell Congress everything about the world situation," he once observed, "they get hysterical. If you tell them nothing, they go fishing."

Seeking a full term in his own right in 1948, Truman would delight audiences by observing, "The Republicans have General Motors and General Electric and General Foods and General MacArthur . . . every general I know is on this list except general welfare."

Also from the 1948 campaign trail: "I heard a fellow tell a story about how he felt when he had to make speeches. He said when he has to make a speech, he felt like the fellow who was at the funeral of his wife, and the undertaker had asked him if he would ride down to the cemetery in the same car with his mother-in-law. He said, 'Well, I can do it, but it's just going to spoil the whole day for me.'"

Truman was a man of traditional values and unswerving loyalties. He once said that three things ruined a man: "Power, money, and women. I never wanted power. I never had any money. And the only woman in my life is up at the house right now."

It's worth noting that Truman should receive credit not only for having a sense of humor himself, but for selecting a vice president—Senator Alben Barkley of Kentucky—who had one as well.

During the debate over an issue where Democrats and Republicans were not holding to their usual party lines, Barkley said, "The situation suggests an old bedchamber scene. There was a spinster who traded in her double bed for twin beds because, she said, 'Every night, I look under the bed to see if there is a man there. With twin beds, my chances are doubled!'"

✯

Barkley used this story to raise questions about an opponent's credibility:

"The parson was all wrought up about the sinfulness of hatred. After holding forth on this un-Christian emotion, he turned to his congregation and asked if anyone present had

fought and conquered the sin of hate. Only one person—a dod-
dering one-hundred-and-four-year-old gentleman—arose.

"'You don't hate anyone, Uncle Bo?'

"'No, I don't, Parson.'

"'That's wonderful. Tell us how you did it.'

"'Well,' he said, 'all of those skunks who done me dirt, all of
them blankety-blanks I hated—they're all dead.'"

Truman was characteristically unrepentant about the most controversial decision of his presidency. "I fired MacArthur because
he wouldn't respect the authority of the president," he said later.
"I didn't fire him because he was a dumb son of a bitch, although
he was, but that's not against the law for generals. If it was, half to
three-quarters of them would be in jail."

Truman never abandoned his populist roots. "I've just been
informed that the Democratic Party, of which I have been an
active member since I was seventeen years old, has gone high hat
and is charging $1,000 for the privilege of sitting with the Presi-
dent of the United States at a dinner," he wrote in 1962. "The
President of the United States represents 180 million people who
have no other person to look after their interests. The President
and the Vice President are the only public officials elected by the
180 million. It is my opinion that 10,000 Democrats at $5 apiece
for the privilege of sitting with and seeing the President as his
guest would be worth 10,000 times that to the Democratic Party.
When the party of the people goes high hat on a cost basis, it no
longer represents the common everyday man—who is the basis of
the Democratic Party."

#8 LYNDON B. JOHNSON

Johnson was a great storyteller. "I remember when I was a little boy, I heard a politician tell a story about a public hanging," the president reminisced. "The sheriff told the condemned man that under the state law he would be allowed five minutes to choose whatever words he cared to speak as his last act. The prisoner responded, 'Mr. Sheriff, I haven't got anything to say, so just get it over with.' But a man way in back in the audience jumped up and said, 'Well, if he doesn't want those five minutes, Sheriff, I'd like to have them. I'm a candidate for Congress.'"

Journalist Hugh Sidey told of a Johnson aide who watched as then-Senator Johnson was conducting a tour of the modest cabin on his Texas ranch that, in Johnson's telling, resembled nothing so much as the famed log cabin in which Abraham Lincoln drew breath. Unfortunately for Johnson, his mother was at his side. "Why, Lyndon, you know you were born in a much better house closer to town which has been torn down," she told her son.

"I know, Mama," responded Johnson, "but everybody has to have a birthplace."

Johnson came by his political instincts naturally. His father, Sam, a member of the Texas legislature, proved a superb instructor. "If you can't come into a roomful of people and tell who is for you and who is against you, you have no business in politics," said Sam Johnson. From his father, LBJ also heard of a candidate running an uphill campaign who had "no more chance than a stump-tailed bull in fly time."

In 1941, LBJ made his first race for the Senate. His opponent was the legendary governor of Texas, Lee "Pass the Biscuits Pappy" O'Daniel. The ultimate consensus politician, O'Daniel declared his platform to be "one hundred percent approval of the Lord God Jehovah, widows, orphans, the Ten Commandments, and the Golden Rule." LBJ narrowly lost. On returning to Washington, he received condolences and some friendly advice from FDR. "I thought you would learn, Lyndon, to sit on the ballot boxes until the final vote is counted," the president told Johnson. "I learned that long ago in New York."

In the 1938 election, the fiery radical congressman from San Antonio, Maury Maverick, was successfully targeted for defeat by Texas conservatives. Thereafter, whenever the Roosevelt White House pressed Johnson to the point that he thought it might endanger his own political base, he had a surefire response. "Don't forget our friend Maury," he would tell Roosevelt. "There's nothing more useless than a dead liberal."

Johnson described an early confrontation between himself and some utility-company executives who were refusing to provide electric power for the farmers in his congressional district. His anger getting the best of him, Representative Johnson told one of the businessmen flat out to "go to hell."

"I felt relieved," Johnson remembered, "and the farmers felt even better." His smile faded, however, when an older man observed that Johnson's outburst had left him back where he'd started. The power company still owned the power lines and the farmers still needed electricity. Thereafter, said Johnson, he was careful never to tell a man to go to hell unless he had the power to make him go there.

Dubbed Landslide Lyndon for his disputed victory in the 1948 Senate election, in which his eighty-seven-vote majority materialized in boss-ridden districts along the Rio Grande, Johnson was naturally sensitive on the subject. At other times he could joke about the race. On one such day he told of a man who, the day after Johnson's senatorial victory, came upon a crying Mexican child in a south-Texas village.

"What are you crying about, Pepe?" asked the man.

"My father came to town yesterday but didn't come to see me," said the child.

"But, Pepe, you know your father has been dead for two years."

"Yes, but my father came to town to vote for Lyndon Johnson; why didn't he come to see me?"

Few men have been happy in the vice presidency, and Lyndon Johnson was no exception. Gracious as ever, leave it to Lady Bird Johnson to find some redeeming feature of that otherwise bleak period in her husband's life. "At least we got our pictures in the papers," she commented.

Another Johnson story concerned a mythical preacher annoyed by a member of his congregation who always snored through the sermon. Finally, the man of God decided to play a little joke. One Sunday morning, while the parishioner was deep in slumber, the preacher said in a low voice, "All of you folks that want to go to heaven, please stand." Everybody stood except the snoring fellow in the front row. When they sat down, the preacher said in a loud voice, "Now all of you folks that want to go to hell, please stand."

That stirred the fellow, who jumped up when he heard the words "please stand." Then he looked around and saw that no one else was standing with him. "Preacher," he finally said, "I don't know what it is we're voting on, but you and I seem to be the only two for it."

Johnson liked to tell of the elder statesman who went to his doctor and complained that he was hard of hearing. The doctor looked him over carefully and asked, "How much are you drinking these days?" The old man said he drank about a pint a day. The doctor said, "Well, if you want to improve your hearing, you are going to have to cut out your drinking." About ninety days later, the fellow went back to his doctor and said that his hearing hadn't improved one bit.

"Have you cut out your drinking?" said the doctor.

"No."

"Well, I can't do anything for you if you won't follow my advice," replied the medical man. "Didn't I tell you when you were here that you should cut out your drinking if you wanted to improve your hearing?"

"Yes."

"Well, why didn't you do it?"

"Doctor," said the old man, "I got home and I considered it, and I just decided that I liked what I drank so much better than what I heard."

One of the rare occasions on which Johnson suffered a putdown involved his young press secretary, Bill Moyers. After Moyers delivered grace over dinner one evening, LBJ complained that he couldn't hear the words of supplication.

"Mr. President," replied Moyers, "I wasn't speaking to you."

A story is told of a White House visit by Israeli prime minister David Ben-Gurion, at the conclusion of which President Johnson reminded his distinguished visitor that being president of 150 million people is no easy job. Ben-Gurion looked up at Johnson sympathetically and told him, "In Israel, it's also not easy being president of two million presidents."

Billy Graham recalls a lunch he and his wife, Ruth, had with President and Mrs. Johnson at the White House as the 1964 Democratic convention was getting under way in Atlantic City. During the meal, Johnson handed the famed evangelist a list of fourteen names and asked, "Now, who would you choose as a running mate?"

Before Graham could respond, Ruth gave him a quick kick in the shins. "You should limit yourself to moral and spiritual advice, not political advice," she told her husband.

"Ruth," said the president solemnly, "that's exactly right."

As soon as the meal concluded and the women left the room, Johnson closed the door, then turned to Graham. "All right," LBJ said, "now what do you *really* think?"

LBJ compared his overwhelming mandate in the 1964 election to the Green Stamps then collected by millions of American shoppers. "You've got this popularity," he explained, "but what value is it if you don't spend it for something worthwhile?" Later on, when Vietnam had sapped much of his electoral strength, Johnson tried to maintain his sense of humor. As he told Democratic congressional candidates, "I'm doing the best I can. It's like the old man in my county that said he felt like a jackass in a hailstorm: he just had to hunker down and take it."

Historian Arthur Schlesinger recorded Johnson's expansive definition of his personal leadership style. "Imagine a football team and I'm the coach, and I'm also the quarterback. I have to call the signals, and I have to center the ball, run the ball, pass the ball. I'm the blocker." He rose out of his chair and threw an imaginary block. "I'm the tackler." He crouched and tackled. "I'm the passer." He heaved a mighty pass. "I have to catch the pass." He reached and caught the pass.

On getting his way—yet again—with Congress, Johnson could barely restrain his delight. "They talk about ca-jolery and persuasion, but this mawning it was sheer horsepower."

In moments of self-pity, Johnson railed against "the Harvards" and others who never gave him credit for his extraordinary legislative accomplishments. "Why don't people like me?" he moaned. To which Dean Acheson bravely replied, "Because, Mr. President, you're not a very likable man."

Ev Dirksen and Lyndon Johnson were old friends from Capitol Hill whose partisan differences never got in the way of their patriotism. Of course, a sense of humor helped. One afternoon Lady Bird Johnson found the two deep in conversation. When she returned several hours later, they were still chatting away. "You don't mind if we denounce you once in a while, do you, Lyndon?" said Dirksen. "You can explain that better than when someone on your side of the aisle denounces you."

On another occasion, Johnson took his old friend to task for some particularly quotable criticisms made of the White House. "Now, why did you say that, Everett?"

"Well, Mr. President," Dirksen replied, "you remember I am the leader of your opposition. And when three dogs come at you, you have to feed them some hamburger."

Dirksen carried a lot of water for the Johnson White House, especially on civil rights, where he helped to break a filibuster blocking passage of the White House bill. One day he confided to his Democratic counterpart, Mike Mansfield, "It's easier to line up votes on your side of the aisle. I have to deal with some real sons of bitches." On the other hand, Dirksen was quick to resent colleagues who sought to silence the flow of *his* spread-eagle oratory. "Sir," he would remark, "you are interrupting the man I most like to hear."

Johnson's prodigious ego inspired an imaginary tale in which Germany's visiting Chancellor Ludwig Erhard allegedly remarked, "I understand, Mr. President, you were born in a log cabin."

"No," replied Johnson, "you have me confused with Lincoln. I was born in a manger."

Then there was the apocryphal story in which the president was pulled over for speeding. Recognizing Johnson, the officer exclaimed, "My God!"

"And don't you forget it!" snapped LBJ.

Johnson Library director Harry Middleton also recalls the first scholarly conference convened at the Johnson Library, which entailed the release of thousands of potentially controversial documents.

"We're opening everything that has anything to do with education, aren't we?" LBJ asked his library director.

"Well, all that *can* be opened," said Middleton. What, Johnson demanded, did that mean? Middleton reminded Johnson that the deed of gift he had signed on turning over his papers to the government contained the usual stipulation that any documents embarrassing to living persons should be kept closed for a decent period.

"Give me an example," said Johnson.

As it happened, Harry had a desktop full of such examples. He began with a colorfully worded memorandum to the president containing a rather scurrilous reference to Oregon congresswoman Edith Green. A silence followed, interrupted by Johnson's angry bark: "Edith's heard worse things than that. Who else is that memo going to hurt?"

Middleton pointed out that the author of the memo, a major Democratic official, might not be thrilled to see his words in print.

"When you were appointed director of the library," Johnson replied, "was there anything in your job description that said you were supposed to hold the Democratic Party together?" After disposing of several other bombshells in similar fashion, Johnson asked accusingly, "Are you going to treat me the same way?"

Choosing his words carefully, Middleton said that the president deserved the same consideration as anyone else. "Good men have been trying to save my reputation for forty years," said Johnson, "and not a damn one's succeeded. What makes you think you can?"

On one occasion Chicago's redoubtable mayor Richard J. Daley visited Johnson in the White House, to sing the praises of a potential U.S. attorney. "He's a great Democrat," Daley began. "He ran for Congress. He was defeated. He's a graduate of Notre Dame, of Harvard. But more than that, Mr. President, let me say with great honor and pride, *he's a precinct captain!*"

Odd as it sounds, Johnson once informed a speechwriter that he was going to address a group of retarded children in the Rose Garden and needed some humor. The dismayed writer went to Press Secretary George Reedy. "Tell him to say, 'I love retarded children—I used to be one myself,'" replied Reedy.

Johnson liked to begin speeches with an unaccustomed touch of verbal humility. "I wish my mother and father might have been here to hear that introduction," he would observe. "My father would have enjoyed it, and my mother would have believed it."

Johnson liked to tell about the poor schoolteacher early in the Great Depression who applied to a school board for employment. He was an impressive candidate, well-spoken and well-informed. The chairman of the school board said as much, then added, "There is some difference of opinion in our community about geography, and we want to know which side you're on. Do you teach that the world is round, or do you teach that the world is flat?"

"I can teach it either way," said the job candidate.

As the war in Vietnam dragged on and his popularity tumbled, Johnson took solace in Mark Twain's story about the time he was walking down a country road in search of a friend's house. At one point he stopped and asked a farmer for directions and was told he had a mile and a half to go. Twain walked on, putting the same question at another household and being told that it was the same mile and a half. This happened three more times. Finally Twain said, "Well, thank God, I'm holding my own."

LBJ liked nothing better than poking fun at his Republican opponents. So he told the tale of an old man who needed a heart transplant and was told of three donor candidates under consideration: an eighteen-year-old athlete, a nineteen-year-old dancer, and a seventy-five-year-old banker. The patient asked the banker's politics. Told that he was a Republican, the patient immediately selected the banker's heart. The operation was carried out successfully. Afterward, people naturally asked the man why it was that he had chosen the banker's seventy-five-year-old heart in preference to that of the younger men.

"I wanted a heart that I knew had never been used," he explained.

Hubert Humphrey might have been joking—and he might have been telling the truth—when he described the phone call he received from Johnson asking him to be his running mate. According to Humphrey, Johnson began the phone call by saying, "Hubert, do you think you can keep your mouth shut for the next four years?"

Humphrey said, "Yes, Mr. President."

"There you go interrupting me again," barked LBJ.

The consummate politician, Johnson once observed, "I seldom think of politics more than eighteen hours a day."

"I have learned that only two things are necessary to keep one's wife happy," said LBJ. "First, let her think she's having her way. And second, let her have it."

To justify budget increases for the missile race with the Russians, Johnson told a group of business leaders the following anecdote. "In 1861, a Texan left to join the rebels. He told his neighbors he'd return soon, that the fight would be easy, 'because we can lick those Yankees with broomsticks.' He returned two years later, minus a leg. His neighbors asked the tragic, bedraggled, wounded man what had happened. 'You said it'd be so easy that you could lick the Yankees with broomsticks.' 'We could,' replied the rebel, 'but the trouble was the Yankees wouldn't fight with broomsticks.'"

Johnson was not afraid of appropriating a good joke. One of his favorites concerned a letter to the postmaster general written by a little boy who had lost his father and whose widowed mother was having difficulty making ends meet. So the boy wrote a letter to the Lord that said, "Dear God, please send Mom $100 to help with the family."

As it happened, the letter wound up on the postmaster general's desk, and he was quite touched by it. So he took a twenty-dollar bill out of his pocket, put it in an official envelope, stuck an airmail stamp on it, and sent it to the little boy. About two weeks later he got a letter back that said, "Dear God: Much obliged for all you have done, but we need another $100. If you don't mind, when you send it to Momma this time, don't route it through Washington, because they deducted 80 percent of it there."

Long before Ross Perot's crazy aunt in the attic, LBJ used a similar analogy to explain his reluctance to discuss progress in Vietnam. "If you have a mother-in-law with only one eye and she has it in the center of her forehead, you don't keep her in the living room."

LBJ and Richard Nixon were longtime political antagonists. Johnson summed up his old foe by comparing him to a Spanish horse, "who runs faster than anyone for the first nine lengths and then turns around and runs backward. You'll see," said Johnson, "he'll do something wrong in the end. He always does."

At a dinner held at Colonial Williamsburg, Governor Winthrop Rockefeller of Arkansas delivered an oration that seemed endless. Johnson was as impatient as anyone else. "I get the feeling that the war in Vietnam," he whispered, "is going to end before this speech."

A restless ex-president, LBJ showered attention on his presidential library. Even before it opened, he insisted that the exhibits address many of the controversies that had engulfed his time in the White House. "I don't want another damn credibility gap," he said. Then he had a brainstorm. "I received some pretty mean mail," he told library officials. "Let's put the meanest letter I ever got in there."

Archivists burrowed through millions of pieces of correspondence, without satisfying Johnson. Eventually the president himself joined the search. After emptying many boxes, Johnson let out a yelp of glee. In his hands was a postcard written by a man in California: "I demand that you, as a gutless son of a bitch, resign as president of the United States."

"You can't get much meaner than that," exclaimed Johnson. The postcard went into the exhibition.

When Johnson died, the longtime director of the Johnson Library, Harry Middleton, instructed library staffers to make a precise count of all those who filed by the president's flag-draped casket. When asked why, Middleton replied, "Because somehow, someday, I know that Lyndon Johnson is going to want to know."

#9 HERBERT HOOVER

Hoover displayed his wry brand of humor in describing his bleak Iowa childhood, including Sabbaths on which he sat noiselessly for hours in a Quaker meetinghouse, his feet not even touching the floor, waiting for the Inner Light to illuminate his life. To be sure, Hoover recalled, he was allowed to read "an improving book" on the Lord's day. As for the rest, "a period of sluggish rest was followed by a Band of Hope meeting, where the lecturer or teacher displayed colored prints of the drunkard's dreadful interior on each stage of his downward path, with corresponding illustrations of his demeanor and conduct."

In his memoirs, Hoover combined nostalgia for his Iowa boyhood with criticism of the New Deal. He recalled picking potato bugs, at one hundred per penny, to buy fireworks for the Fourth of July celebrations that enlivened even sober Quaker households. "If that wage still prevails," Hoover noted in his memoirs, "it ought now to be adjusted to the commodity dollar and is entitled to a hearing by the Labor Board. It may be that the use of arsenic on bugs has created technological unemployment in the firecracker industry. If so," he asserted with an obvious swipe at

FDR's agricultural policies, "the recent remedy would be to dig up the potatoes while they are young."

In October 1897 a London mining firm asked its American representative to recommend a candidate with thirty-five years of age and seven years of experience to work the newly capitalized mines of Australia. The twenty-three-year-old Hoover inflated his credentials, grew a mustache to make himself look older, and acquired a natty tweed outfit suitable for his London interview.

He got the job. Two years later, the friend who had talked him into buying the suit received it back in the mail. "Since you like this damn thing," wrote Hoover from the hellish heat of Australia's outback (which he described as being "three yards inside civilization"), "take it. I haven't worn it yet." Australia, concluded Hoover, was a land of "red dust, black flies, and white heat."

As a young man, Hoover had been forced to spend four months of each year surveying bleak Western landscapes on horseback. As a result, he wrote whimsically, "I've often wondered if a mistake had not been made when the horse was created. Geologically there had been camels before the horse. Why was the horse not given the camel's tank, and thus save watering him more than once a day? Centipedes had been made. Why not have given a horse six short legs and thus he would be nearer the ground and have a better gait? Fish scales had been invented long before. Why not have put scales on the horse instead of hair, so that he could not annoy you all the time fighting flies?"

During Prohibition, Hoover made no protest when his wife, Lou, emptied out their wine cellar, which boasted the finest port in California. Said Hoover, "I don't have to live with the American people, but I do have to live with Lou."

As secretary of commerce, Hoover the angler helped restock the nation's streams with half a billion baby fry. He reported on the problem with a whimsy rarely glimpsed in public. "America is a well-watered country," he told the Izaak Walton League, of which he had become president, "and the inhabitants know all the fishing holes. The Americans also produce millions of automobiles. These coordinate forces of inalienable right, the automobile and the call of the fishing hole, propel the man and boy to a search of all the water within a radius of 150 miles at weekends alone. He extends it to a radius of 500 miles on his summer holidays. These radii of operations . . . greatly overlap. Not surprisingly," concluded Hoover, "the time between bites has become longer and longer, and the fish have become wiser and wiser."

During World War I, Hoover returned home at President Wilson's invitation to run the American Food Administration under the battle cry "Food Will Win the War." Soon Hoover had millions of his countrymen dining on whale steaks and chewing sugarless gum, living in unheated houses and baking Over The Top bread to government specifications. Sugar bowls disappeared from restaurant tables, and a popular verse summed up the deprivations of a nation cheerfully "Hooverizing" its way to victory:

> I cannot thank you for your bread
> Because there wasn't any.
> Nor any butter, either, though
> Its substitutes were many.
> But your pecan and fig croquettes;
> Your muffins, flour and eggless;
> Your beefsteak, raised in windowbox;

Your mock duck, wing and legless;
Your near-fish, wheedled from oatmeal;
Your butteries, from apple;
Your catsup salad, dressed with lard;
Your porkless, parsnip scrapple
Composed a menu so conserved
That Mr. Hoover'd better
Commend my cheer in sending you
This meatless, wheatless letter!

There was even a Food Administration valentine:

I can Hooverize on sugar,
And on meat and fuel, too;
But I'll never learn to Hooverize
When it comes to loving you!

In 1920 there were efforts in both parties to nominate Hoover, the man who had fed Belgium and earned worldwide renown as the Great Humanitarian. On the other hand, at least one shrewd observer noted that Hoover, an engineer by training, lacked any flair for politics. "He's like a cat with water," she noted. "He doesn't like the amusing indirectness of getting things done in a political way, and that means he won't like Congress!"

Hoover was too self-effacing to excel at campaigning. Someone likened his handshake to "a flag at half-mast on a windless day."

On learning of the birth of his granddaughter, Hoover cracked, "Thank God, she doesn't have to be confirmed by the Senate."

Few men have had a more difficult time of it in the White House. Hoover tried to put it in humorous perspective. "Many years ago I concluded that a few hair shirts were part of the mental wardrobe of every man," he wrote. "The President differs only from other men in that he has a more extensive wardrobe."

On at least one occasion, a fish got the president into hot water, so to speak. It happened when a group of Maine lawmakers presented the White House with a fat, fresh salmon, snagged in the waters around Bangor. Before a beaming congressman could be photographed with its presumably delighted recipient, the scaly gift was dispatched to the executive kitchen. Edward Starling, chief of Hoover's Secret Service detail, was later forced to sew the fish's head back on. Not without consolation; "Maine," Starling noted proudly afterward, "did not go Democratic for three years."

Following his disastrous defeat in the 1932 campaign, Hoover made the best of things, informing an audience that he had been offered many learned explanations for his loss. Having made a lengthy scientific analysis of the situation himself, said Hoover, he could report, "As nearly as I could learn, we did not have enough votes on our side."

Hoover had his own, not terribly flattering, definition of the presidency. It was, he said, "nothing but a twenty-ring circus—with a whole lot of bad actors."

Hoover liked to say that a modern president can engage in only two pursuits with the expectation of privacy. One was fishing, and the other was prayer—and no man can pray all the time. "A fisherman must be of contemplative mind, for it is often a long time between bites," wrote Hoover. "Those interregnums emanate patience, reserve, and calm reflection—for no one can catch fish in anger, or in malice. He is by nature an optimist, or he would not go fishing; for we are always going to have better luck in a few minutes or tomorrow. All of which creates a spirit of affection for fellow fishermen and high esteem for fishing."

What's more, Hoover continued, "Fishermen are gregarious. Otherwise, the mighty deeds of a day or of a year ago or of ten years ago would go unsung. No one but fishermen will listen to them. Therefore, as two or three are gathered together, the spiritual vitamins of faith, hope, and charity have constant regeneration. And we need all in these years of creaking civilization."

Finally, Hoover summed up the philosophical appeal of his favorite pastime. Fishing, he said, is a lesson in democracy, "for all men are created equal before fishes."

Soon after Pearl Harbor, Hoover told a friendly journalist that his opposition to American involvement in the war before the Japanese attack had made him something of a political leper. "Truth has never been timed to suit the tastes of the people who do not want to hear it," he added. "In view of the way the Preacher was treated, it would seem that the Sermon on the Mount was badly timed."

After leaving the White House, Hoover immersed himself in literary pursuits, including an all-purpose indictment of enemies at home and abroad, which in one early version was to feature no fewer than fifteen critical blunders of statesmanship. Years later, an overnight guest at Hoover's suite at New York's Waldorf Towers discovered the elderly ex-president scribbling furiously at his desk long before dawn. What could he possibly be doing at such an hour, the intruder asked.

"I'm making my Roosevelt book more pungent," said Hoover.

It took a while, but eventually Hoover even managed to crack wise about the most painful chapter in his life. "Once upon a time my political opponents honored me as possessing the fabulous intellectual and economic power by which I could create a worldwide Depression all by myself."

Like many old men, Hoover had trouble sleeping at night. Invariably, he would rise from his bed and plant himself at a desk, from which he answered literally thousands of letters each year. Many came from small children. One youthful correspondent wrote inquiring about presidential travel. Hoover replied that presidents must travel to learn what people have on their minds, and to explain their own policies. Moreover, executive travel had greatly improved for presidents since the times when George Washington required five or six days to go from New York to Washington.

"Presidents today can do it now in one hour by jet," said Hoover. "But jets go over the heads of the people—like some of the speeches."

One child wrote asking Hoover for an autograph. "I was delighted to see that you are not a professional autograph hunter," Hoover responded. "Once upon a time one of those asked me for three autographs. I inquired why. He said, 'It takes two of yours to get one of Babe Ruth's.'"

Then there was the young lady who informed Hoover she had not yet been born when he was in the White House and confessed her ambitions to be a doctor.

"My dear Kathleen," responded the former president. "You were saved a lot of trouble by not being born earlier. I'm glad you want to be a doctor and not President. We do not have enough doctors, and there seems to be a sufficient number of candidates for President."

The May 1947 Gridiron Club dinner coincided with the first Republican Congress in a generation. Seated a few feet from Harry Truman, Hoover consciously refrained from gloating over this development, or its implications for 1948. As Hoover put it, "To elaborate would be an indelicate implication that I am seeking a recruit to my exclusive union of ex-presidents."

It was ninety-one degrees in the shade in July 1957 when Hoover joined his friend Harry Truman for the dedication of the Truman Library in Independence, Missouri. Afterward Hoover was approached by an admirer wanting to know exactly what ex-presidents did with their days.

"Madame," said Hoover, "we spend our time taking pills and dedicating libraries."

"You will discover," Hoover wrote Richard Nixon in January 1961, "that elder statesmen are little regarded by the opposition party until they get over eighty years of age and are harmless."

Classroom Humorists

#10 WOODROW WILSON

Wilson's father, a Presbyterian minister, was himself something of a wit. The president liked to relate the story of the Reverend Mr. Wilson's chance meeting with a member of his congregation. "Your horse looks very well, Mr. Wilson," said the parishioner. "Much better than you do."

"Yes," replied Dr. Wilson. "You see, I keep my horse, but I am kept by my congregation."

As a young man unhappily studying law (which he found "monotonous as hash"), Wilson dreamed of a statesman's career. Forever taking his emotional temperature, Wilson once observed that "the hardest enterprise in the world is to rule one's spirit. After that, to rule a city is a pastime!" The private Wilson was far more appealing. "It may shock you," he wrote his first wife during their courtship days, "but I'm afraid it will not, to learn that I have the reputation amongst most of my kin and certain of my friends for being irrepressible . . . in select circles, as a maker of grotesque addresses from the precarious elevation of chair seats, as a wearer of all varieties of comic grimaces, as a simulator of sundry, unnatural burlesque styles of voice and speech, as a lover of farces—even as a dancer of the can-can!"

It was true. Within the bosom of his family, Wilson could discard his mask of formality and enter gleefully into charades, convulsing his daughters as he became a pompous dowager slithering in a feather boa or a stuffy Englishman fingering his monocle. Wilson loved vaudeville shows, nonsense songs, and the tricky patter of Gilbert and Sullivan. His lusty rendition of the "Duke of Plaza Toro" was on a scale with his much requested imitation of a rubber-legged drunk.

As president of Princeton, dealing with an obstreperous faculty, Wilson foreshadowed his later problems with Congress. According to legend, the strong-willed administrator asked his board of trustees point blank, "Why, how can I democratize this college unless I have absolute authority?"

Many people thought Wilson distant and his manner chilly. Reminded by a Princeton colleague that there were two sides to every question, Wilson shot back, "Yes, a right side and a wrong side." William Allen White said that shaking the president's hand was like grasping a five-cent mackerel in a brown paper bag. Wilson himself claimed to have two natures—one Irish, one Scotch. The first was quick, generous, impulsive, passionate, "anxious always to help and to sympathize with those in distress" . . . the other "canny, tenacious, cold, and perhaps a little exclusive.

"I tell you, my dear friend, that when these two fellows get to quarreling among themselves, it is hard to act as umpire between them." In the meantime, he sighed, "I have the uncomfortable feeling that I am carrying a volcano about with me."

Wilson did not hesitate to exploit his looks, or lack of them, for political advantage. Indeed, when running for governor in 1910, he readily conceded that his Republican opponent had the advantage of him in this category. At the same time, he added, "It is not always the most useful horse that is most beautiful. If I had a big load to be drawn some distance, I should select one of those big, shaggy kind of horses, not much for beauty, but strong of pull."

In 1912, William Jennings Bryan was a reluctant convert to Wilson's cause. Four years earlier someone had asked the Great Commoner, "How does Woodrow Wilson strike you for the vice presidency?"

"First rate," said Bryan. "He strikes me every chance he gets."

Wilson had no illusions concerning his grassroots popularity, especially when compared to that of the ineffable Theodore Roosevelt. "He appeals to their imagination; I do not," said Wilson. "He is a real, vivid person, whom they have seen and shouted themselves hoarse over, and voted for, millions strong; I am a vague, conjectural personality, made more up of opinions and academic prepossessions than of human traits and red corpuscles."

Wilson loved puns and limericks. One of his favorite verses proved ironic in light of the events engulfing his administration in its second term:

> War is rude and impolite
> And quite upsets the nation,
> It causes weeks and months of strife
> And years of conversation.

Something of a conservative in his younger days, by the time he ran for president in 1912, Wilson was firmly identified with the progressive movement. He delighted audiences with his biting description of a conservative as "someone who just sits and thinks, mostly sits." Alternatively he defined conservatism as a policy of "make no change and, when in doubt, consult your grandmother."

At one point Theodore Roosevelt denounced Wilson as a weak leader in thrall to the sound of his own voice. The target of this assault professed indifference. "What's the use of wasting good serviceable indignation on him?" asked Wilson.

The day before Wilson's 1913 inaugural, the streets of Washington were filled with hundreds of female protesters carrying banners that read, "Tell Your Troubles to Woodrow." Woodrow, apparently, had too many troubles of his own to pay much attention to the demonstrators. Eventually four suffragettes chained themselves to the White House fence to protest the president's failure to argue for self-determination at home with the same fervor he showed in foreign lands.

With true Southern courtliness, Wilson wished to invite one freezing group of suffragettes inside the White House for some hot tea. Edith Wilson, a traditionalist to the core, was immovable. "But it's cold out there," said the president. Finally head usher Ike Hoover was dispatched, over the first lady's protest, to extend an offer of presidential hospitality. The women rejected the olive branch and took their punishment—fifteen days in jail for disturbing the peace.

No one ever accused Wilson of indecisiveness. "The beauty about a Scotch-Irishman is that he not only thinks he is right, but knows he is right."

Once, asked whether he was binding himself to any particular course regarding Panama Canal tolls, Wilson replied, "I am not binding myself on anything. I am ready to break loose at any minute." Asked on another occasion if he had found a successor for his State Department counselor, the president said, "It is not difficult to find one; it is difficult to select one. We haven't selected one yet."

Wilson had difficulty adjusting to his new life as "a public character." Sometimes, he told reporters, he felt as if he should stand before a mirror and see "if he could not look like a monument." On second thought, being a monument might be better "than being shaken hands with by the whole of the United States."

Wilson once declared of the presidency that it requires "the constitution of an athlete, the patience of a mother, the endurance of the early Christian."

Long a student of government, Wilson was nevertheless appalled by the reality of life in Washington. He liked to say that every man who came to the nation's capital either grew or swelled. He was also frustrated by the city's resistance to change, observing, "If you want to make enemies, try to change something."

Wilson professed indifference to a second term. "If you think too much about being reelected," he once explained, "it is very difficult to be worth reelecting."

During World War I, Wilson became the first mass-marketed president, thanks to newsreels and other newly developed instruments of communication. To assist hungry European allies, Wilson created the United States Food Administration, entrusted to Herbert Hoover. The new agency promoted Meatless Mondays, and Wheatless Wednesdays. On Gasless Sundays, President and Mrs. Wilson were driven to church in a horse and carriage.

In time, a flock of well-publicized sheep appeared on the White House lawn, their wool auctioned off to benefit the Red Cross. The first lady, whose immoderate pride in her Native American ancestry had earned her the not altogether flattering nickname of Pocahontas, was redubbed Little Bo Peep. Unfortunately, her economy drive cost more than it saved when the sheep began devouring White House shrubbery and flowers.

"Sometimes people call me an idealist," said Wilson during World War I. "Well, that is the way I know I am an American. America is the only idealistic nation in the world."

Wilson's bad stomach was just one of many ailments that dogged him throughout adult life. Referring to his chronic indigestion, the president said that he suffered from turmoil in Central America. In response, White House physician Cary Grayson prescribed a regimen of golf, oatmeal, and a daily raw egg in orange juice. Wilson enjoyed his time on the links and made no complaint about the breakfast cereal. The raw egg was a different story. Every time he drank one, said the president, he felt as if he were swallowing a newborn baby.

The 1916 election was among the closest in American history. Not for three days did Wilson know for sure that he had been reelected. His vice president, Thomas Marshall, thought winning was winning. "'Tis not so deep as a well, nor so wide as a church door," said Marshall, "but 'tis enough, 'twill serve!"

Wilson was hardly the only president for whom reading newspapers was a daily irritant. Still, the former college professor claimed that nothing in the press could get under his skin. "I've been accustomed to reading fiction."

Wilson voiced another familiar lament when he suggested a certain discrepancy between events as described by journalists and as *experienced* by the president. "Every morning I pick up the paper and see that there are all sorts of friction," said Wilson, "if not already in existence, then just about to be created. I must be exquisitely lubricated," he added smilingly, "for I do not feel any friction."

Wilson termed his revolutionary legislative program the New Freedom. His critics called it Universal Regulation.

On the subject of Wilson, his usually genial predecessor could be tart indeed. "I felt certain that he would not recognize a generous impulse if he met it on the street," said Taft.

Theodore Roosevelt, predictably, was even more scathing. Among other things, TR called the professorial Wilson "a Byzantine logothete."

Wilson's high-minded approach to the issues attracted support from unlikely quarters. Thomas Edison was a lifelong Republican, yet he endorsed the president for reelection in 1916. "They say Wilson has blundered," explained the great inventor. "Well, I reckon he has, but I noticed he always blunders *forward*."

Wilson was a man of strong emotions, restrained only at considerable cost. "If I wrote what I think of that man," he said of an opponent, "it would have to be on asbestos."

Wilson was an incorrigible punster. On learning that Virginia's Senator Carter Glass had attained an important position in the Methodist Church, the president expressed surprise that the Methodists would raise a glass so high.

A true golf addict, Wilson nevertheless mocked the game as "an ineffectual attempt to put an elusive ball into an obscure hole with implements ill adapted to the purpose."

During World War I, the Wilson administration introduced the concept of daylight saving time. According to a popular story, an elderly White House chef, told to have dinner ready at seven, answered irritably, "By what time—Wilson's time or Christ's time?" Everybody in the room laughed. Wilson's own face broke into a smile, but only for a moment. "That is irreverent," he said.

When the White House doctor took away his pet medicines, Wilson, ever the wordsmith, accused him of being a "therapeutic nihilist."

On the day after his wedding to the former Edith Bolling Galt, the fifty-nine-year-old president was seen walking through a railroad car singing a popular song of the period—"Oh, You Beautiful Doll." For her part, the second Mrs. Wilson proved herself fiercely loyal. As late as 1961 she could refer to her husband's archenemy, Henry Cabot Lodge, as "that stinking snake."

At his last cabinet meeting, Wilson was asked his postpresidential plans. "I am going to try to teach ex-presidents how to behave," he said. Then the old schoolmaster added, "There will be one very difficult thing for me, however, to stand, and that is Mr. Harding's English."

Wilson spoke no foreign language. "To know English properly," he explained, "has kept me so busy all my life that I haven't had time for anything else."

At the Versailles Peace Conference, Wilson was sucked into the whirlpool of Old World controversies. At one point French premier Clemenceau was arguing the case for harsh treatment of defeated Germany, including crushing reparations and taxes on the vanquished nation. Wilson staunchly objected to all this.

"You have a heart of steel," said Clemenceau.

"But I have not the heart *to* steal," retorted Wilson.

Wilson made little effort to conceal his contempt for lesser minds. From his father, a Presbyterian minister, Wilson had learned to think—and speak—precisely. "Shoot your words straight at the target," he had been told. Referring to senators who opposed his League of Nations, Wilson said that he might someday "burst merely by containing restrained gases . . . when the lid is off, I'm going to resume my study of the dictionary to find adequate terms to describe the fatuity of these gentlemen with their poor little minds that never get anywhere but run around in a circle and think they're going somewhere."

Wilson's chief antagonist was Henry Cabot Lodge, a stiff-necked Brahman from Massachusetts who liked to be known as the Scholar in Politics. Lodge despised Wilson, his diplomatic notewriting—even his "Woodrovian style." According to Lodge, the latter "might be good enough for Princeton, but it would never pass muster at Harvard."

Wilson thought little of modern public relations devices, especially the increasingly common practice of designating certain weeks for specific movements—for example, Be Kind to Animals Week, Clean-up Week, Better Homes Week, National Air Week. Indeed, said Wilson, "There should be a week designated for people to mind their own business."

Following Wilson's stroke in the fall of 1919, he became an invalid. Hostile legislators suspected Mrs. Wilson of running the country. Declared Senator Albert B. Fall of New Mexico, "We have petticoat government!" To test his theory, Fall invited himself and a delegation of his colleagues to the White House. There they found the stricken president in bed, yet far from enfeebled.

In fact, Wilson seemed so hearty that it unnerved Fall into murmuring, "Mr. President, I am praying for you."

"Which way, Senator?" chuckled Wilson.

On his deathbed, reduced to liquid nourishment and little of that, Wilson produced another limerick:

> A wonderful bird is the pelican
> His bill will hold more than his belly can.
> He can take in his beak
> Enough food for a week
> I wonder how in the hell he can.

At one point in the president's illness, it was suggested that Wilson might feel comfortable if one of his doctors shaved off his beard. Indeed, he was told, in olden days doctors were really barbers.

"And they are barbarous yet," said Wilson.

#11 JAMES GARFIELD

As a young Ohio schoolteacher, Garfield was unnerved by the unceasing "thump and bang" of the classroom. "It is indeed trying to my patience and also to my stomach to have so many little ones about me." He even wrote a verse summing up his frustrations:

> Of all the trades by men pursued
> There's none that's more perplexing
> Than is the country pedagogue's—
> It's every way most vexing.

The classic self-made man, Garfield spoke from experience when he said, "A pound of pluck is worth a ton of luck."

In 1854, Garfield was admitted to Williams College in western Massachusetts, where he immediately fell under the spell of its charismatic president, Mark Hopkins. Years later, he discharged his debt to Williams by claiming, "The ideal college is Mark Hopkins on one end of the log and a student on the other."

"I am a poor hater," Garfield once acknowledged. During Reconstruction, when emotions were running high, Congressman Garfield told a friend, "I am trying to do two things—be a radical and not be a fool—which, if I am to judge by the exhibitions around me, is a matter of no small difficulty."

At the same time, Garfield quickly became convinced that President Andrew Johnson was either "crazy or drunk with opium." His greatest fear was that Johnson would ally himself with Southern rebels and Northern copperheads to regain control of Congress and undo the victory won on the battlefield. "Then woe to liberty, and the public debt," said Garfield.

Garfield had little use for those who would flout fiscal ortho-doxy by inflating the currency. Garfield detested paper money, which he called "the printed lies of the government." To be sure, some temporary pain might result from returning to the gold standard, but consider the alternative: "A man's hand is hope-lessly shattered," Garfield imagined, "it must be amputated or he dies; but the moment the surgeon's knife touches the skin, he blubbers like a boy and cries, 'Don't cut it! Take away the knife!' The natural laws of circulation were amputated by and by."

"Honesty *is* the best policy," Garfield insisted, "even when running for Congress." The independent-minded Garfield saw himself as undertaking a political experiment, "to see whether a man can think and speak his convictions. . . . If it fails," he added nonchalantly, "the world is wide and we are free."

One of Garfield's closest friends, Jeremiah Black, was also among the unlikeliest. Black had defended Andrew Johnson at his impeachment trial. Before the war, he had served in Buchanan's cabinet as attorney general. Above all, Black was a hard-shell Democrat. Asked why he didn't become a Republican, Black replied, "I believe in a hell!"

Garfield could not be said to lack for partisan instincts himself. Taking to the stump in 1866, he denounced President Johnson and his allies–"the unwashed, unanointed, unforgiven, unrepen-tant, unhung Rebels of the south." Who, asked Garfield, were the Democrats?

"Every rebel guerrilla and jayhawker, every man who ran to

Canada to avoid the draft, every bounty jumper, every deserter, every cowardly sneak that ran from danger and disgraced his flag, every man who loves slavery and hates liberty, every man who helped massacre loyal Negroes at Fort Pillow, or loyal whites at New Orleans, every Knight of the Golden Circle, every incendiary who helped burn northern steamboats and northern hotels, and every villain, of whatever name or crime, who loves power more than justice, slavery more than freedom, is a Democrat and an indorser of Andrew Johnson."

For all Garfield's disdain of Johnson, he entertained lukewarm feelings toward impeachment. For one thing, Johnson's Senate trial seemed anything but dramatic. "We have been wading knee-deep in words, words, words, for a whole week," Garfield complained, "and are but little more than half across the turbid stream." And then, as if previewing a future impeachment proceeding, Garfield theorized "that if the choice were given to some of our fiercest impeachers to speak and lose their case—or to keep silent and win it—they would instantly decide to read a six-hour speech to an unwilling audience."

In an age of flowery rhetoric, Garfield sought to persuade rather than inflame. "The age of oratory has passed," he announced. "The newspaper, the pamphlet, and the book have abolished it. Only plain speaking—argument and fact that may be printed—are of any great value now."

Like most other politicians of his day, Garfield resented the constant pressure of office seekers. A congressman, he once declared, is nothing but a target for such pests, "who infest every public place, and who meet you at every corner, and thrust their papers in your face as a highwayman would his pistol."

In 1872, liberal Republicans disgusted by Grant's performance as president rallied around newspaper editor Horace Greeley, who quickly revealed himself to be a political disaster. "The movement was a revolution," quipped Garfield, "but the revolution has revolted." The reform movement that wound up with a standard-bearer such as Greeley recalled for him the fable of the beautiful woman who ended up with the tail of a fish.

"I would say Grant was not fit to be nominated, and Greeley is not fit to be elected," said Garfield.

Adamant as ever in opposing inflation, Garfield despaired of holding the line against Western agrarians. "We might as well address the patients in the lunatic asylum on finance," he muttered, "as to hope to change the tone of the House at present." Let other congressmen yield to the popular clamor. "I will not vote against the truth of the multiplication table," insisted Garfield.

When politics became all but unbearable, Garfield lost himself in his books. He was especially fond of the works of Jane Austen, which he much preferred to current fiction. "The novel of today," he declared in words uncannily prescient, "is highly spiced with sensation, and I suspect it results from the general tendency to fast living, increased nervousness, and the general spirit of rush which seems to pervade life and thought in our times."

Garfield boasted of substantial budget reductions, leading one Democratic opponent to poetically mock his claims of economy:

> Though the mills of the gods grind slowly,
> yet they grind exceedingly small,
> but the mills of your committees
> do not grind at all.

During one tough reelection campaign, Garfield turned down challenges to debate. "Let my enemies draw their own crowds," he said. "I draw mine." As the campaign ground on, however, he became less restrained. Following one particularly brutal tongue-lashing of his opponent, Garfield observed, "I doubt if he knew, when I left him, whether he was hash or jelly."

Like many middle-aged men, Garfield felt the weight of time. Birthdays had once seemed to be milestones, he joked, but now they resembled nothing more than tombstones.

A Republican rival eager to replace Garfield in the House submitted a petition signed by 140 voters who agreed with the candidate that "the time has come *when the office ought to seek the man*." Soon after, Garfield wryly observed, "as a commentary on this doctrine, Northway is riding through the district to give the office a chance to find him."

"I long ago made a resolution that I would never permit myself to let the presidential fever get any lodgment in my brain,"

Garfield once commented. "I think it is the one office in this nation that for his own peace no man ought to set his heart on." This didn't prevent friends of John Sherman, the Ohio senator whom Garfield was pledged to support for the presidency in 1880, from accusing the congressman of not working hard enough to elect Sherman.

Garfield responded by telling a story attributed to Lincoln, concerning a boy seen making a church out of mud.

"Why don't you make a preacher, too?" Lincoln had asked.

"Lawsy," said the boy, "I ain't got mud enough."

Garfield, apparently, didn't have mud enough to make the "Ohio Icicle" Sherman into an acceptable candidate.

No sooner was he nominated than Garfield received some friendly advice from his fellow Ohioan, President Rutherford B. Hayes. The GOP candidate should refrain from speeches for the balance of the campaign. Better yet, he ought to "sit cross-legged and look wise until after the election." Above all, Garfield should observe "an absolute and complete divorce from your inkstand . . . *no letters to strangers,* or to anybody else *on politics.*"

Once elected, Garfield had to choose a cabinet. Originally he had hoped to foster national unity by including at least one Southerner. This proved no small task. "One by one, my Southern roses fade," the president-elect sighed, frustrated in his search for "a magnolia blossom that will stand our Northern climate."

Grant objected to the reforming policies of James Garfield, who refused to appoint to office Grant partisans known as Stalwarts. "Garfield," complained Grant, "has shown that he is not possessed of the backbone of an angleworm." As the storm rose, one senator contrasted Garfield the porcupine with Rutherford Hayes the dove. For his part, Garfield was unapologetic. "It had better be known," he blurted out, "whether the president is the head of the government, or the registering clerk of the Senate."

As befitting a former college professor, Garfield installed a three-thousand-volume library in the White House. As a release from the pressures of office, he translated Latin odes and enjoyed the poetry of Tennyson and Shakespeare. Still, he could not escape the horde of office seekers who stretched down Pennsylvania Avenue. A friend of the president's said that White House corridors resounded to "the sound of beasts at feeding time."

Garfield had a neat put-down for the office seekers who tormented him. "They open their mouths for a horse," he said, "but are perfectly willing to settle for a fly."

Garfield lingered for weeks after being wounded by an assassin's bullet. But even on his deathbed, he managed a bit or two of wry humor. One day, he asked for a pencil and a clipboard, then scrawled his name and wrote under it a Latin phrase, *Strangulatus pro Republica*—"tortured for the Republic." At other times, his mood was anything but sunny. This was hardly surprising, given his diet of lime water and oatmeal. On being told that the great Indian Sitting Bull was starving himself in captivity, Garfield snapped, "Let him starve." A moment went by, and the president had a still more wicked thought. "Oh, no," he said, "send him my oatmeal."

Moving Up

#12 George Bush

In his first race for Congress, in 1966, Bush hinted at his later disdain for political pigeonholing. "Labels are for cans," he said.

At the 1988 GOP convention, Bush made his famous No New Taxes pledge. Two years later, he reversed course, reluctantly accepting a tax increase as the price of deficit reduction. This was political dynamite, but the president only made things worse by joking about it. Reporters who confronted him during one of his morning jogs saw Bush point at his backside and blurt out, "Read my hips."

In his 1988 campaign acceptance speech, Bush rebutted his critics by acknowledging that, while he might lack eloquence, "I learned early that eloquence won't draw oil from the ground." More humorously, Bush promised to be fair to the other side. "Tonight I'll try to hold my charisma in check."

During the campaign Bush also joked about his blue-blood lineage. At one point he insisted that his ancestors had landed at

Ellis Island when the *Mayflower* made a pit stop en route to Plymouth. "My people," Bush said, "were the ones waving the Bloomingdale's shopping bags."

When it came to the art of public persuasion, Bush often seemed to be in the shadow of his predecessor (I know how he feels—neither of us has ever been called a Great Communicator). As Bush put it, "Fluency in the English language is something I'm often not accused of."

To his credit, Bush could laugh at his distinctive use of the language. In the midst of an economic recession, he explained, "We're enjoying sluggish times and not enjoying them very much."

Bush the optimist refused to accept gloomy forecasts for the future. "If anyone tells you that America's best days are behind her," said the president, "they're looking the wrong way."

In introducing his 1992 State of the Union address, Bush joked about his oratorical prowess. "With all the high expectations for this speech, I wanted it to be a big hit," he said. "But I couldn't convince Barbara to deliver it."

In his *Campaign Comedy: Political Humor from Clinton to Kennedy,* Gerald Gardner made much of the campaign one-liners Bush didn't use to deflate Clinton's 1992 economic program . . .

"Governor Clinton's economic plan looks to me like 'broccoli economics.' He makes it sound good, but I find it hard to swallow."

"The president is the commander in chief, not calculator in chief."

"You look at the taxpayer's wallet like another cheeseburger to be gobbled down."

To Bush's credit, his stump speech did include the following zinger:

"Bill Clinton keeps talking about change. But if his economic policies go into effect, change is all you'll have left in your pockets."

In the wake of his reelection defeat, President Bush recalled the stunning upset of Winston Churchill back in 1945. At that time Churchill had said, "I have been given the order of the boot." And that, said Bush, "is the exact same position in which I find myself today."

In one commencement speech, former President Bush half-threatened to spend forty-five minutes talking about the Federal Reserve Board, followed by half an hour on the gold standard. He then relented, inspired by a story he attributed to the Reverend Billy Graham. It concerned a long-winded speaker whose oration droned on endlessly, until a man at the head table picked up his shoe, threw it at the speaker's podium, missed his target, and struck a lady in the front row instead.

"Hit me again," she said, "I can still hear him."

#13 WILLIAM HOWARD TAFT

Taft's problems in the presidency were foreshadowed from the outset. Frigid weather in March 1909 forced his inauguration to be moved indoors, a departure from tradition that would not be repeated until Ronald Reagan's second inaugural in 1985. Over breakfast that morning with the outgoing president, Theodore Roosevelt, Taft belittled his promotion. "Even the elements protest," he chuckled. Much later Taft would observe, "I always knew it would be a cold day when I became president of the United States."

Taft hid his love of travel under a common presidential lament. "I have come to the conclusion," he once declared, "that the major part of the president is to increase the gate receipts of expositions and fairs and bring tourists into the town."

A maladroit politician, Taft showed himself to be more candid than shrewd. Early in 1908 he was asked, "What is a man to do who is out of work and starving?"

"God knows," replied Taft. "I don't." Apparently this was a genetic defect. Many years later Taft's son, Robert, was pressed for his solution to high prices and postwar shortages of meat. "Eat less," said Taft, a real chip off the old block.

In the White House, Taft developed a reputation for putting off decisions. William Jennings Bryan dubbed him the Great Postponer.

Taft counted among his friends the millionaire railroad lobbyist turned senator Chauncey Depew of New York. The irreverent Mr. Depew once approached the rotund president, placed his hand on Taft's stomach, and asked, "What are you going to name it when it comes, Mr. President?"

Unfazed by such audacity, Taft quickly responded, "Well, if it is a boy, I'll call it William. If it's a girl, I'll call it Theodora. But if it turns out to be just wind, I'll call it Chauncey."

The 1912 Republican convention, held in Chicago, was bitterly divided between Taft supporters and those loyal to former president Theodore Roosevelt. At one point Taft supporters had ten thousand handbills printed, announcing that, at seven-thirty Monday evening, Colonel Roosevelt would walk on the waters of Lake Michigan.

Unhappy from his first day in office, Taft quickly tired of the presidential routine. "It seems to be the profession of a president simply to hear other people talk," he complained.

Taft jokingly quoted the old saying that while men are different, all husbands are alike. "The same idea may be paraphrased with respect to congressmen. Congressmen are different," he said, "but when in opposition to an administration, they are very much alike in their attitude and in their speeches."

According to his military aide, Colonel Archibald Butt, Taft was so lacking in musical sensibility that he had to be nudged to stand whenever a band played "The Star Spangled Banner."

Taft frequently mortified his associates by regularly nodding off in public after meals. His own wife dubbed him Sleeping Beauty.

One lawmaker told the 350-pound chief executive after he awoke from one such nap, "Mr. President, you are the largest audience that I ever put entirely to sleep in all my political experience."

Especially embarrassing was a cabinet dinner at which Taft asked for music to be played on the White House Victrola. Before the first piece ended, he was sound asleep. He woke briefly and requested a second number, only to resume his slumber. The officers of state listened to the performance, accompanied by the president's loud snoring. This was too much for Secretary of the Treasury MacVeagh, who put on a rousing march with the promise that "it will wake anyone but a dead man."

Still Taft slept. "He must be dead!" MacVeagh told a presidential aide.

"The other day I gave up my seat in the streetcar," said the president famed for his girth. "And three ladies sat down."

Once stuck at a railroad station, and learning that the train would only stop if a number of passengers wished to come aboard, Taft telegraphed to the conductor, "Stop at Hicksville. Large party waiting to catch train."

On the surface, Taft appeared cheerfully unselfconscious about his bulk. After he and his brother seated themselves for a theatrical performance one night, the president remarked, "Horace, if this theater burns, it has got to burn around me."

Long before 1912, disappointed Republicans agreed with the doggerel writer who summed up the Taft presidency:

Teddy, come home and blow your horn,
The sheep's in the meadow, the cow's in the corn.
The boy you left to tend the sheep
Is under the haystack fast asleep.

It was a far cry from Taft's 1908 campaign, waged against William Jennings Bryan.

"I don't believe Bryan is the man he used to be," remarked one GOP senator.

"No, and he never was," added a colleague.

The Taft administration earned a special niche in White House history, owing to the presence of Pauline, the family cow, which gave milk highly prized by the thrifty Tafts. Pauline even inspired a skit at the Gridiron Club, where the placid creature was favorably contrasted with Roosevelt's teddy bear. Asked what he planned to do with the cow, the vice president of the club replied, "Milk her. That is what all the politicians are trying to do to her owner."

Taft's four years in the White House were marred by dispiriting press criticism. "Don't worry over what the newspapers say," Taft told friends. "I don't. Why should anyone else? I told the truth to the newspaper correspondents—but when you tell the truth to them, they are at sea."

Theodore Roosevelt dismissed his onetime friend as "a president who meant well but meant well feebly."

Not long after his defeat in the 1912 presidential election, Taft delivered a wry valedictory. His theme: What Are We to Do with Our Former Presidents? With his tongue firmly in cheek, Taft proposed "a dose of chloroform or . . . the fruit of the lotus tree" as a means to protect his countrymen from the troublesome fear that the occupant [of the nation's highest office] could ever come back. What's more, said Taft, such decisive methods would relieve the former president himself "from the burden of thinking how he is to support himself and his family, fix his place in history, and enable the public to pass on to new men and new measures."

As for the suggestion made by some that former presidents should become ex officio members of the Senate, Taft was dubious. "If I mean to go and disappear into oblivion," he chuckled, "I prefer to go by the chloroform or lotus method. It's pleasanter and less drawn out."

Taft said that leaving the presidency was like being let out of jail. But how was he to make a postpresidential living? When it was suggested that he might occupy a chair of law at Yale, Taft said that he was afraid that a chair might not be adequate, but that if the university would provide a sofa of law, it might be all right.

#14 John Adams

As unyielding as the stony soil of his Quincy farm, Adams harbored few illusions about human perfectibility. Indeed, it had been his sour lot in life to discover "that Men find Ways to persuade themselves to believe any Absurdity, to submit to any Prostitution, rather than forgo their Wishes and Desires. Their Reason becomes at last an eloquent Advocate on the Side of their Passions and [they] bring themselves to believe that black is white, that Vice is Virtue, that Folly is Wisdom, and Eternity a Moment."

Like some other New Englanders, Adams was not notably modest about his region's contributions to mankind. As he put it, "Boston Town Meetings and our Harvard College have set the universe in motion."

Adams cherished not only his country's independence, but his own. "I do not say when I became a politician," he once commented, "for that I never was."

Following Washington's victory at Yorktown, even Adams's friends were uneasy over news that the sour-tempered New Englander had been appointed to serve on the Peace Commission. "He hates Franklin," noted Jefferson, "he hates Jay, he hates the French, he hates the English. To whom will he adhere?" The answer, of course, was the United States, the only thing Adams loved on a par with his family and his farm.

Though a religious man, Adams did not proselytize. "I never write or talk upon divinity," he told Abigail. "I have had more than I could do of humanity."

Even members of Adams's official family questioned the president's political gifts. In the words of James McHenry, Adams's secretary of war, "Whether he is spiteful, playful, witty, kind, cold, drunk, sober, angry, easy, stiff, jealous, cautious, confident, close, open, it is always in the wrong place or to the wrong person."

Much given to self-pity, Adams also had a thick vein of jealousy. "Mausoleums, statues, monuments, will never be erected to me," he told a friend after the Revolution. On another occasion, he predicted that the history of America's struggle for independence "will be one continued lie from one end to the other. The essence of the whole will be that Dr. Franklin's electrical rod smote the earth and out sprang General Washington. That Franklin electrified him with his rod—and thenceforward these two conducted all the policy, negotiations, legislatures, and war."

It has never been easy to be vice president; imagine being in Washington's shadow. In moments of pique, Vice President Adams was even known to refer to his majestic superior as Old Muttonhead. To what did Washington owe his special status? Adams thought he knew. First, there was his great height—"like the Hebrew sovereign chosen because he was taller by the head than the other Jews." Then, there was the matter of Washington's Virginia birth—"as Virginian geese are all swans." Finally, said Adams, there was Washington's genius for silence. "Here you see I have made out ten talents without saying a word about reading, thinking, or writing."

Still, Adams was downright reverential toward Washington when compared with less exalted politicians. He labeled Alexander Hamilton "the bastard brat of a Scots peddler." In the Continental Congress, Adams scorned John Dickinson as "a great fortune and piddling genius." Another politician from his own Bay State was dismissed as "a pretty little warbling canary bird." He opposed banks as aristocratic opponents of the farmer and workingman. "A bank that issues paper interest is a pickpocket or a robber," said Adams.

Adams was a sort of eighteenth-century Don Rickles, spewing insults for the sheer pleasure of it. Still, his hatred of Hamilton was absolutely genuine. The former secretary of the treasury, wrote Adams, "like the worm at the root of the peach, did labor for twelve years, underground and in darkness, to girdle the root, while all the axes of the anti-Federalists, Democrats, Jacobins, Virginia debtors to English merchants, and French hirelings, chopping as they were for the whole time at the trunk, could not fell the tree."

Benjamin Franklin famously observed that Adams was "always an honest man, often a great one—but sometimes absolutely mad."

As the wife of the vice president, Abigail Adams registered a familiar complaint. "It is next to impossible to get a servant to the highest to the lowest grade that does not drink, male or female. I have at last found a footman who appears sober," she wrote from New York, "but he was born in Boston."

In the fall of 1790, the new government pulled up stakes and left New York for Philadelphia. The Adamses were disappointed in their new home, Bush Hill, which had no bushes and only a few inadequate storerooms and closets. Uprooted from Manhattan, Mrs. Adams in particular missed the soothing sweep of the Jersey wheatfields and the majestic river at her door. "The Schuylkill is no more like the Hudson," she said, "than I to Hercules."

Himself a lawyer, Adams was not above repeating an unflattering bit of verse about his fellow attorneys:

> You ask me why Lawyers so much are increased
> Tho much of the Country already are fleeced
> The Reason I'm sure is most strikingly plain
> The Sheep are oft sheared yet the Wool grows again.

In the wake of his defeat for reelection in 1800, Adams told one of his sons, "If I were to go over my life again, I would be a shoemaker rather than an American statesman."

In March 1801, Adams stormed out of Washington rather than attend the inauguration of his onetime-friend-turned-bitter-political-enemy Thomas Jefferson. On arriving at Quincy two weeks later, he discovered a hundred loads of seaweed in the barnyard. On reflection, wrote Adams, he had made "a good exchange . . . of honors and virtues for manure."

"Ennui," he told a friend, "when it rains on a man in large drops, is worse than one of our northeast storms; but the labors of agriculture and amusement of letters will shelter me."

Thomas Jefferson admired his friend's stubborn refusal to march in party ranks. Said Jefferson, Adams "is as disinterested as the being who made him."

To forestall American involvement in Europe's wars, Adams courageously dispatched a diplomatic mission headed by Charles C. Pinckney to England. Many opposed the move; some resorted to scurrilous allegations about the president's motives. When critics whispered that Pinckney's real mission was to procure two girls apiece for himself and his White House sponsor, Adams thought the whole thing too ridiculous to take seriously.

"I do declare upon my honor," wrote the president, "if this be true, General Pinckney has kept them all for himself and cheated me out of my two."

"No man who ever held the office of president," Adams observed, "would congratulate a friend on obtaining it. You will make one man ungrateful, and a hundred men his enemies, for every office he can bestow."

A voracious reader, Adams advised anyone who would listen that "you will never be alone with a poet in your pocket."

In his old age, Adams achieved true wisdom. "Human nature cannot bear prosperity," he told his son John Quincy. "It invariably intoxicates individuals and nations. Adversity is the great reformer. Affliction is the purifying furnace." He urged his ambitious son to retire from the political arena, even if that meant "you should be obliged to live on turnips, potatoes, and cabbage, as I am. My sphere is reduced to my garden, and so must yours be." As for pursuing high reputation, Adams thought it no more important "than the grunting of a bagpipe."

Adams affected tranquillity in his old age, foreseeing "what all ages have foreseen, that poor earthly mortals can foresee nothing, and that after all our studies and anxieties, we must trust Providence." But the old fires burned. On learning that his grandson wished to pursue a naval career, Adams advised him to aim higher: "You should leap at the moon and seize her by the horns when necessary, as your grandfather and father have done before you."

In the last weeks of his life, Adams received a visit from Noah Webster, who naturally enough inquired after the former president's health.

"I inhabit a weak, frail, decayed tenement," responded Adams, "open to the winds and broken in upon by the storms. What is worse, from all I can learn, the landlord does not intend to repair."

#15 GEORGE WASHINGTON

Mark Twain declared himself to be a greater man than Washington, for Washington couldn't tell a lie, and he could.

A shrewd student of human nature, Washington once observed, "Few men have virtue to withstand the highest bidder."

Those who knew Washington also knew the source of his majestic, even forbidding, public persona. Said one playmate from his youth, "Of the mother I was ten times more afraid than I ever was of my own parents . . . whoever has seen the awe-inspiring air and manner so characteristic of the father of his country will remember the mother as she appeared when the presiding genius of her well-ordered household, commanding and being obeyed."

At the age of twenty-three, gauging his chances like a colonial ward heeler, Washington contemplated running for Virginia's House of Burgesses. "Sound their pulse, with an air of indifference and unconcern," he instructed a friend on the scene, "without disclosing much of *mine.*" On election day, Washington suffered a crushing defeat at the hands of voters from whom he withheld the customary alcoholic inducements. When he next sought office in thirsty Winchester County, Washington made sure the liquor flowed generously. Profiting from defeat would become his hallmark, whatever the field of battle.

Early in the Revolution, Washington enjoyed a laugh at the expense of "valiant New Englanders" who aspired to be "chimney-corner heroes." A Virginia lady writing her friends in 1777 noted that when "General Washington throws off a Hero and takes up a chatty agreeable Companion, he can be downright impudent sometimes, such impudence, Fanny, as you and I like."

No one who took part in the rout of the British at Princeton would ever forget the sight of their commanding officer, Washington, on horseback pursuing the fleeing redcoats and shouting, "It's a fine fox chase, boys."

When entertaining the president of Congress after the battle of Princeton, General Washington served wine in cups, the maker of which, someone observed, had recently become a Quaker preacher. Washington said it was too bad the man had not turned preacher before making the cups.

During the Revolution, Washington and his army suffered from chronic shortages of weapons, clothing, supplies, and above all, money. When financier Robert Morris declared he had his hands full, Washington replied sardonically, "I wish he had his pockets full, too."

On another occasion Washington was dining in front of a fireplace in use. When the heat became too great, he moved to another place around the table. Someone reminded him that generals ought to be able to stand fire.

"Yes," agreed Washington, "but it does not look well for a general to receive the fire behind."

At Yorktown, victorious Americans were understandably eager to exalt their victory over the British. Leave it to Washington to dampen the party. Riding up and down his army's lines, the general forbade any unseemly demonstrations, declaring, "Posterity will huzzah for us."

Washington was at best a reluctant politician. On the eve of his first presidential inauguration, he told his old friend Henry Knox, "My movements to the chair of government will be accompanied by feelings not unlike those of a culprit who is going to the place of his execution."

After the war, Washington grew increasingly impatient with the weak confederation tolerated by states unwilling to part with their sovereignty. "Influence is no government," he wrote in October 1786.

The stable at Mount Vernon housed Royal Gift, an enormous jackass presented to Washington by an admiring Spanish monarch for breeding purposes. Disdaining thirty-three American fillies prepared as a harem, Royal Gift appeared to his owner too aristocratic to sample such "republican enjoyments" as the New World offered. Even as Washington, desperate for cash to support his official household, advertised the jack's services in Virginia gazettes at $10 per mare, he wrote humorously that the creature was "too full of royalty to have anything to do with a plebeian race."

Suffering the consequences of his fame, Washington found himself pursued endlessly by portrait painters. "*In for a penny, in for a pound*, is an old adage," he wrote in 1785. "I am so hackneyed to the touches of the painters' pencils, that I am now altogether at their beck; and sit 'like Patience on a monument' whilst they are delineating the lines of my face. It is a proof, among many others, of what habit and custom can accomplish. At first I was as impatient and as restive under the operation as a colt is of the saddle. The next time I submitted very reluctantly but with less flouncing. Now no dray horse moves more rapidly to his thill than I do to the painter's chair."

As the most famous man on earth, Washington could not avoid the steady stream of visitors who turned Mount Vernon into what he called a well-resorted tavern. His house bulged with visitors. "I rarely miss seeing strange faces," confided the president, "come, as they say, out of respect for me. Pray, would not the word *curiosity* answer as well?"

At the Constitutional Convention in Philadelphia, Washington rarely participated in debates. He broke this rule, however, when he disagreed with Benjamin Franklin over a motion to limit the size of any standing army to three thousand men. Washington dismissed the idea out of hand. He *could* support the motion, said the general, but only on condition that the Constitution also required foreign powers wanting to attack the United States to limit *their* armies to the same size.

Not long ago, a poll in *Newsweek* revealed that 14 percent of all American preschoolers think that George Washington is still in the Oval Office. The rest of us just wish he were.

Washington was anything but a Great Communicator. In fact, he was painfully awkward when delivering a speech. Elevating this shortcoming to the level of principle, the first president once advised a nephew elected to the Virginia Assembly against becoming "a babbler."

We now know that Washington never wore wooden teeth. Instead, he used state-of-the-art dentures carved from hippopotamus tusk. No Washington myth is easier to dismiss than the story of the first president's hurling a coin across the Potomac—if only because no man was less likely to throw away a dollar. As the thrifty Washington put it, "Many mickles make a muckle."

As president, Washington hosted weekly levees, rigidly choreographed receptions where bow was substituted for a handshake and Washington made small talk dressed in black velvet ordered from Europe at $5 a yard. When journalists criticized his bow, the president's feelings were hurt. After all, he told friends, his greetings were bestowed indiscriminately. "Would it not have been better to throw the veil of charity over them, ascribing their stiffness to the effects of age or to the unskillfulness of my teacher, than to pride and dignity of office, which God knows has no charm for me?"

Martha Washington was no more fond of life in New York, the nation's first capital. "I live a very dull life and know nothing that passes in the town," she confided in October 1789. "I never go to any public place. Indeed, I think I am more like a state prisoner than anything else; there are certain bounds set for me which I must depart from, and as I cannot do as I like, I am obstinate and stay at home a great deal."

One way or the other, it is a lament with which each succeeding first lady could sympathize.

Mrs. Washington played hostess at Friday-night receptions, which were portrayed by Abigail Adams as "usually very full of the well born and well bred. Sometimes . . . as full as her Brittanick Majesties Room, and with quite as handsome ladies, and as polite courtiers . . . they chat with each other, swish about, fine ladies show themselves, and as candlelight is a great improver of beauty, they appear to great advantage."

Washington was determined to avoid being sucked into partisan politics. "Men's opinions were as various as their faces," he liked to say, and where their motives were pure, no more to be questioned than nature itself.

Frugal by inclination as well as necessity, Washington complained that other families were able to entertain more liberally than he could on one-tenth his salary. So he did what unhappy hosts have done since time began—he blamed the servants. Specifically, the steward of his household, one John Hyde, of whom Washington wrote, "I strongly suspect that nothing is brought to my table of *liquors, fruit,* or *other things* that is not used as *profusely* at his."

Washington traveled extensively as president, well aware that he was the new country's only unifying agent. His diary is full of crisp observations, by no means all of them flattering to his hosts. In one North Carolina town, for example, he was greeted by "as good a salute as could be given by one piece of artillery." Wherever he went, Washington was escorted by admirers; in time, the dulling of the incense of adulation got on his nerves. "It is not easy to say on which road—the one I went or the one I came—the entertainment is most indifferent," Washington wrote in his diary, "but with truth, it may be added that both are bad." Worse were the dust storms that swirled around his carriage thanks to the formal escorting parties that insisted on accompanying Washington whenever he reached a settlement.

Could Washington tell a lie? You bet. "Having suffered very much by the dust yesterday," he once wrote, not feeling in the least guilty over his falsehood, "and finding the parties of Horse and a number of other gentlemen were intending to attend me a part of the way today, I caused their inquiries respecting the time of my setting out to be answered that I should endeavor to do it before eight o'clock; but I did it a little after five, by which means I avoided the inconveniences above mentioned."

Only by practicing the arts of deception could Washington enjoy a few hours to himself, riding Southern roads instead of inhaling them.

If it's any consolation to modern presidents, not even the father of his country could get everything he wanted from Congress. On at least one memorable occasion the U.S. Senate rejected Washington's nomination of a South Carolinian named John Rutledge to be chief justice of the Supreme Court on the grounds of insanity. In fact, the only evidence of Rutledge's insanity was his disagreement with a majority of the U.S. Senate.

As has often been remarked, every action Washington took established a precedent for his successors. This made him understandably cautious. Initially he took literally the Constitution's instruction to seek congressional "advice and consent." Early in his first term he went before lawmakers to discuss administration policy toward Native Americans. Before any action could be taken, however, a senator from Pennsylvania moved to refer the entire business to the appropriate congressional committee.

"This defeats every purpose of my coming here," exploded Washington. Soon after he withdrew, vowing that he would be damned rather than face the U.S. Senate again. This is one precedent many of his successors wish they could follow.

#16 THOMAS JEFFERSON

"The man who fears no truths has nothing to fear from lies," asserted Jefferson. This did not mean that he was wholly insensitive to the scandalous rumor-mongering that filled the gutter press of his day. At one point, Jefferson declared the most truthful part of newspapers to be their advertisements. What's more, he said, "The man who reads nothing at all is better educated than the man who reads nothing but newspapers."

For those who think negative campaigning is a modern invention, consider this newspaper story predicting the consequences of Jefferson's election in 1800: "Unrestrained by law, or the fear of punishment . . . neighbors will become enemies of neighbors, brothers of brothers, fathers of their sons, and sons of their fathers. Murder, robbery, rape, adultery, and incest will be openly taught and practiced, the air will be rent with the cries of distress, the soil soaked with blood, and the nation black with crimes." And President Clinton took offense at being called Slick Willie!

Jefferson shared the general distrust of early America of political factions. "If I could not go to heaven but with a party," he once wrote, "I would not go there at all." He was equally suspicious of political ambition. "Whenever a man has cast a longing eye on offices," said Jefferson, "a rottenness begins in his conduct."

Trained as a young man in the law, Jefferson had no illusions about that talkative profession. "Were we to act but in cases where no contrary opinion of a lawyer can be had," he said, "we should never act."

A man of the people, Jefferson wryly observed that he had seen no evidence that men's honesty increased with their riches.

"No man will ever bring out of the presidency the reputation which carries him into it," Jefferson commented. By and large, he was right.

A true conservative who liked to say that the best government was the least government, Jefferson was even more outspoken in portraying the potential dangers of bureaucracy—what he called "too many parasites living on the labor of the industrious."

Finding activity the best antidote for whatever ailed him, emotionally or otherwise, Jefferson coolly informed one friend, "No laborious person was ever yet hysterical."

Himself insatiable for knowledge and culture, Jefferson imposed a strict regimen on his daughter Martha: "8:00–10:00, practicing music; 10:00–1:00, dance one day, draw another; 1:00–2:00, draw on the day you dance, and write the letter the next; 3:00–4:00, read French; 4:00–5:00, exercise yourself in music till bedtime, read English, write, etc."

In those days before women pursued careers of their own, Jefferson had his own reasons for urging such a rigorous schedule. Combining his gift for mathematics with his insight into human nature, Jefferson calculated the odds at about one in fourteen that his daughter would marry "a blockhead."

As his country's ambassador to France, Jefferson was asked by a friend's daughter to undertake a rather personal errand on her behalf. His response is worth quoting in full: "Mr. Jefferson has the honor to present to Mrs. Smith and to send her the two pair of Corsets she desired. He wishes they may be suitable, as Mrs. Smith omitted to send her measure . . . should they be too small, however, she will be so good as to lay them by a while. There are ebbs as well as flows in this world. When the mountain refused to come to Mahomet, he went to the mountain."

Elected vice president in 1796, Jefferson chose to make the best of a bad lot. "It will give me philosophical evenings in the winter," he said of his new position, "and rural days in summer."

According to the scholar Paul M. Zall, an expert on the humor of America's Founding Fathers, at the dinner celebrating his first inauguration as president, Jefferson was approached by a gentleman from Baltimore, who asked permission to wish him joy.

"I would advise you," said the new president, "to follow my example on nuptial occasions, when I always tell the bridegroom I will wait till the end of the year before offering my congratulations."

In his seventies, Jefferson likened romance to a colt. "It must be broken before it is safe to ride."

#17 BILL CLINTON

When it was revealed during the 1992 campaign that Vice President Quayle intended to be "a pit bull" in the coming campaign, Clinton quipped, "That's got every fire hydrant in America worried."

Clinton was brainy enough to be self-deprecating about his brains. On one occasion, after being introduced as the smartest of the Democratic presidential candidates, he replied, "Isn't that like calling Moe the most intelligent of the Three Stooges?"

President Clinton's speeches often lacked the jokes and stories that peppered President Reagan's addresses. He confessed to a Democratic dinner, "I used to have a sense of humor, but they told me it wasn't presidential, so I had to quit."

At the Statuary Hall luncheon following his inauguration in 1993, President Clinton got a laugh from all those present— including me—when he began his remarks by saying, "Just when [Speaker Foley] wished me well in untangling my relationships with Congress, my head, almost as if by magic, tilted in Senator Dole's direction."

When the Dallas Cowboys came to the White House in 1996 to be recognized for their Super Bowl victory, Clinton said, "This is the only thing that happens at the White House as regularly as the State of the Union Address. In some ways, it's better. It's shorter—and there's no Republican response."

While visiting American troops in the Balkans, Clinton drew appreciative laughter when he told the soldiers, "The military promised you square meals. And when you get your eggs each morning, you know the military has kept its commitment."

Clinton once described Warren Christopher, his famous gray and buttoned-down secretary of state, as "the only man ever to eat presidential M&M's on Air Force One with a knife and fork."

At a St. Patrick's Day ceremony in 1996, the president poked fun at Vice President Gore's environmental image when he responded to a gift of a bowl of shamrocks by saying it had two benefits. "First, this being an election year, I need all the shamrocks I can get. And second, this is the one day of the year when I am more green than the vice president."

Upon receiving a laudatory introduction from one of his cabinet members, the president told his listeners about "Clinton's Third Law of Politics," which was "Whenever possible, be introduced by someone you have appointed to high position. Their objectivity is stunning."

Clinton did share with a New Orleans audience this classic story about the boring minister who decided to step up his preaching style: "He worked and worked for months to develop a sermon that he felt was the finest, most barn-burning, most emotion-generating sermon he had ever delivered. And he filled the church one day and, boy, he gave a stem-winder. Nobody could believe it. It was magnificent. And the punch line was "I want everybody who wants to go to heaven to stand up right now." And the whole congregation leapt to their feet, except one lady in the front row who sat stone still. And she hadn't missed a Sunday in forty years; the most faithful member of the church wouldn't get up. He was crestfallen. He said, "Sister Jones, don't you want to go to heaven when you die?" And she jumped right up. She said, "Oh, I'm sorry, Preacher, I thought you were trying to get up a load to go right now."

Although often reluctant to use humor in speeches outside of Washington, D.C., President Clinton proved that he was blessed with great timing and talented writers during his annual appearances at the White House Correspondents Dinner and the Radio and Television Correspondents Association Dinner in the nation's capital. Here are some of his best lines.

In a 1995 appearance at the Radio and Television Correspondents Association Dinner, the president listed new ways in which money could be saved to help solve the ongoing budget crisis. Included in his proposals:

> Vice President Gore, ever the humble public servant, suggested that this year we could save money by doing away with the White House Christmas tree, and we could just hang the ornaments on him.
>
> Consolidating White House staff by replacing fifteen thirty-year-olds with five ninety-year-olds.
>
> Providing corporate sponsorships for government, like making February 12 Lincoln-Mercury's birthday.
>
> Combining the Bureau of Alcohol, Tobacco and Firearms with both the Bureau of Fisheries and the Interstate Trucking Commission. We're going to call it the Department of Guys.

Clinton closed his remarks at that dinner by joking about his proclivity to give long speeches, saying, "Well, I could go on like this forever, but you know that, don't you?"

The 1994 dinner of the Radio and Television Correspondents marked the fiftieth anniversary of that organization, and President Clinton took the occasion to wax historical:

> In your association's first year, 1944, Franklin Roosevelt delivers more of his fireside chats over the radio. It's not much different today, except today you insist that the president sit directly on the logs.
>
> Following a reliable source, just hours after the polls closed in 1948, network news airs the very first televised interview with President-elect Thomas Dewey.
>
> In 1952, Eisenhower says he will go to Korea, and the first question from the press is about the seating arrangements on the plane.
>
> In 1960, researchers discover that people who watched the Kennedy-Nixon debate on television thought Kennedy won. People who listened to the debate on radio thought, "When in the hell am I going to get a television?"

Clinton went on to joke about his well-documented battle with food, joking, "People say to me, 'Remember Harry Truman: If you can't stand the heat, get out of the kitchen.' It's the only room in the house I never want to leave."

The 1997 Radio and Television Correspondents Dinner and White House Correspondents Dinner were only two weeks apart. On both occasions, President Clinton found a gold mine of "lame duck" material in that he had recently injured his knee when he tripped over a stair at the home of professional golfer Greg Norman. Also in the news at that time was the parachute jump made by former president Bush. Clinton joked:

> Until recently, I had planned out a really dramatic entrance to the [Radio and Television Correspondents] dinner—and then George Bush stole my thunder. This guy is seventy-two years old, and he jumps out of a plane at ten thousand feet and lands without a

scratch. I fall six inches and I'm cooped up for six months. It's ridiculous.

At various times throughout the president's remarks, Mike McCurry, the White House press secretary, handed the president notes. The president opened them up and read the following to the appreciative audience:

> According to wire reports, former president Bush has just bungee-jumped off the Seattle Space Needle. . . .
> You'll be pleased to know that former president Bush has just successfully jumped the Snake River Canyon on a rocket-powered motorcycle. Now he's just taunting me. . . .
> Ladies and gentlemen, former president Bush has just had himself manacled, placed inside a padlocked trunk, and submerged off the coast of Kennebunkport. The clock is ticking. Our prayers are with him.

The president also joked how different television channels covered his knee surgery:

> C-SPAN, of course, provided live uninterrupted coverage of my injured knee, while C-SPAN 2 devoted full coverage to my other knee. Within an hour of the accident, CNN had composed ominous theme music, and put up a graphic, "Breaking News, Breaking Knees." . . . MSNBC immediately proclaimed itself the state-of-the-art global interactive command center for all leg-related news. ESPN broke into the North Carolina–Colorado basketball game with a breathless bulletin that Greg Norman was just fine. PBS kept interrupting coverage of my knee for pledge drives. For every hundred-dollar donation, you got a commemorative X ray of my leg. [Conservative pundit] Bob Novak went on *Crossfire* to argue the positive aspects of debilitating knee injuries for Democrats. And then, there was MTV. All they wanted to know was, did I wear a hospital gown or pajamas?

★

At the White House Correspondents Dinner two weeks later, Clinton returned to the subject of his knee, helpfully giving the press advance notice of some upcoming mishaps:

> While engaging in some volunteer work tomorrow in Philadelphia, I will be on the receiving end of a painful encounter with a ball peen hammer. . . . On May twenty-second, I will be visiting the home of Tiger Woods to celebrate his recent victory in the Masters. Please be advised: There is a loose brick on the patio. On July 8, during the fifth inning of the baseball All-Star game in Cleveland, I will attempt to catch a foul ball.

At that dinner, Clinton also joked about how past presidents engaged in the fine art of "spinning" the press:

> I had the National Archives send over some yellowed transcripts to make this point. For example, here's some good news from the Hoover administration: housing starts were up in the third quarter of 1931. Said a senior adviser to the president, "These Hoovervilles reflect a commitment to private initiative instead of paternalistic big government. The president is proud they bear his name.
>
> "Then in 1814, a White House official disputed the idea that the burning of the White House was a setback for the Madison administration. 'Yes, fire did consume the mansion,' he said. 'But it was in desperate need of renovation anyway—and this salutary effort by the British actually saves us time and taxpayers' money.'"

And You Always Thought
They Were Dull

#18 Dwight Eisenhower

One of Eisenhower's favorite stories involved the Quaker farmer back in Indiana who would never use the name of the Lord in vain. But one day his mule, who was hitched to a hay wagon, wouldn't budge an inch. The farmer patiently tried every known bit of coaxing without any success. Finally he reached the end of his rope. "Mule," he said calmly, "thee knows that because of my religion I cannot beat thee, or curse thee, or abuse thee. But, mule," he continued, "what thee doesn't know is that I can sell thee to an Episcopalian."

Appearing on the CBS series *See It Now* with Edward R. Murrow in the spring of 1952, Eisenhower compared political office to a hammock: "It's hard to get into and even harder to get out of gracefully."

"Only two kinds of problems ever reach my desk," remarked Eisenhower, "those marked urgent and those marked important—and I spend so much time on the urgent, I never get to the important."

In his book, *At Ease: Stories I Tell My Friends,* Eisenhower described a Columbia University dinner he attended as the school's president. "There were three previous speakers," he recalled. "Each had gone on at considerable length, and as the evening threatened to become morning, I decided to set aside my own text. When the time came to speak, I stood up, said that every speech, written or otherwise, had to have punctuation. I said, 'Tonight, I am the punctuation—the period,' and sat down. It was one of my most popular addresses."

There was one good thing about being president, said Ike: "Nobody can tell you when to sit down."

"The War Department moves in mysterious ways," cracked this five-star general, "its blunders to perform."

The president's brother Milton recalled a commencement ceremony in the spring of 1955 at which Ike was scheduled to give the main address. Storm clouds were forming as the participants donned their robes for the outdoor event. Milton's distress was plain to see. Asking his brother for advice, he was told, "Milton, I haven't worried about the weather since June sixth, 1944 [D day]."

Having twice defeated the erudite "egghead" Adlai Stevenson, Ike was entitled to his prejudices. "An intellectual is a man who takes more words than necessary to tell more than he knows," he said.

Following his September 1955 heart attack, Ike was advised by doctors to pursue healthier routines. No fewer than four physicians urged him to avoid tobacco in all its forms. The president listened politely, then noted that all four were themselves smoking. "I remarked pointedly that I had used no tobacco for more than six years," he would write, "and wondered why I should be in bed with a heart attack while they were up and working, apparently hale and hearty."

Ike was a good deal more sophisticated politically than he let on. After all, few men knew more about leadership or how to boost morale than the commander of Allied forces in World War II. Nor did he hesitate to lecture candidates with whom he appeared. "Now here's what you do," he liked to say. "Get out there. Don't look so serious. Smile! When the people are waving at you, wave your arms and move your lips, so you look like you're talking to them."

Eisenhower's imperious chief of staff, Sherman Adams, didn't make many jokes, but he inspired a few. One suggested that while it would be terrible if Eisenhower were to die, and Vice President Nixon were to take his place, it would be even worse if Sherman Adams died and *Eisenhower* became president.

Employing what later scholars called his "hidden hand," Eisenhower helped grease the skids for Wisconsin's Senator Joseph McCarthy, whose anticommunist crusade had become an embarrassment to the White House. Following McCarthy's censure by

the Senate in December 1954, Eisenhower declared, "McCarthy-
ism is now McCarthywasm."

At the time of the Army-McCarthy hearings in the spring of
1954, Eisenhower told his cabinet, "There is a phrase that a man
is known by the friends he keeps. The other side of the coin is that
a man is known by the enemies he makes. I read the last speech
of Senator McCarthy. He said in that that we should have nothing
to do with any nation that trades with the Reds. If he's against
that, I'm for it."

As befitting a man who spent much of his life in the barracks,
Ike was not above using rough language to make a point. Asked
why he didn't take a more vigorous public role in opposing Senator Joseph McCarthy, Eisenhower replied, "I just won't get into
a pissing contest with that skunk."

Eisenhower's cabinet began each meeting with a prayer, usually delivered by Secretary of Agriculture Ezra Taft Benson. One
day, Ike entered the cabinet room engaged in lively discussion
with a colleague. The conversation continued well into the time
allotted for the meeting. At this point, cabinet secretary Max
Rabb slipped the president a note reminding him that they had
overlooked the usual moment of silent prayer.

"Oh, God damn it," said Ike, "we forgot the silent prayer."

On the first anniversary of his 1952 nomination as the Republican candidate for presidenct, Eisenhower was presented a set of
fishing lures by his cabinet. Press Secretary James Hagerty set out

to demonstrate the gift, only to get one of the fishhooks entangled in what the official cabinet minutes describe as "an embarrassing location." Finally, Agriculture Secretary Benson intervened and Hagerty was cut loose.

Eisenhower said he had more fun out of the incident than at any time since his brother Milton sat on a fishhook.

Asked to name his biggest mistake while in office, Ike replied forthrightly, "I made two, and they're both sitting on the Supreme Court."

Eisenhower had a healthy skepticism about the Washington bureaucracy. Once, when Treasury Secretary George Humphrey boasted that his department had only three public relations experts, the president replied, "Get out a special medal for the Treasury Department!" On second thought, he added, "If they haven't gotten them hidden under some other name, I'm a monkey's uncle!"

Eisenhower once ordered Secretary of Defense Charles Wilson to undertake a quick survey of his workforce. Anticipating resistance, Ike cut it off briskly. "Don't tell me you can't do it in Defense, I invented the system," the president told Wilson. "You can ask for fat, bald-headed majors, and they'll come tumbling out of the IBM machine."

In the midst of an Oval Office discussion one afternoon, the president pointed to a squirrel outside his glass porch door. The creature kept jumping up and hitting the glass. Eisenhower laughed and said, "That just proves what I've been saying around here. This is a nuthouse—oh, well, that squirrel has a lot more sense than some of the visitors I've had lately."

Ike took his card games seriously—especially bridge. Whenever a partner of his would make a mistake, Eisenhower would tell of the colonel who cut into a subordinate's apology with the remark "No explanation is necessary because none would be satisfactory."

Eisenhower liked to extol the virtues of what he called Modern Republicanism. In his case, *modern* was a synonym for *moderate*. "The middle of the road is all of the usable surface," he explained. "Both extremes—right and left—are in the gutters."

In Ike's last year in the White House, a reporter observed, "Sir, do you realize that on your upcoming birthday you will be the oldest president ever to serve?"

Eisenhower smiled and said, "I believe it's a tradition in baseball that when a pitcher has a no-hitter going for him, nobody reminds him of it."

Few presidents look forward to vacating the office; certainly Ike didn't. Throughout the winter of 1960–61 he watched glumly as stands were erected in front of the White House for the inauguration of his successor. Said Eisenhower, "I feel like the fellow in jail who is watching his own scaffold being built."

At the 1964 Republican convention in San Francisco, Congressman Bob Mathias, a liberal Republican, was outraged over the impending nomination of Barry Goldwater. Mathias planted himself in the back of the hall. At the podium former president Eisenhower delivered a rousing speech. It apparently went over Mathias's head. Pondering the Goldwater menace, he was heard to mumble, "This would never have happened if Eisenhower were still alive."

#19 GERALD FORD

It's well known that President Ford never aspired to the nation's highest office, but hoped instead to become Speaker of the House of Representatives. Nevertheless, even he wasn't completely immune to Potomac fever, as he acknowledged at a 1968 Gridiron Dinner. Sometimes late at night, said Ford, as he drove past 1600 Pennsylvania Avenue, he imagined a little voice in his head saying, "If you lived here, you'd be home now."

During the 1976 campaign, Ford needled his opponent over the issue of defense spending. He reminded audiences of Teddy Roosevelt's famed aphorism, "Speak softly and carry a big stick." Jimmy Carter had it all wrong, said Ford. The Georgian wanted "to speak loudly and carry a flyswatter."

Ford joked about his unlikely ascent to the nation's highest office, claiming that the Marine Band was a little confused. "They don't know whether to play 'Hail to the Chief' or 'You've Come a Long Way, Baby.'"

Early in his presidency, Ford had an outdoor swimming pool built with privately raised funds. At the same time, he acknowledged, "You don't need to have the pool at the White House to get in deep water."

Ford once said of his vice president that Nelson Rockefeller was the only taxpayer who could balance the federal budget with his mad money.

Ford also was a good sport when it came to some of the not-so-sporting things said by Washington sophisticates. Returning to his alma mater, he began a speech by declaring, "It's a great pleasure to be at the Yale Law School Sesquicentennial Convocation . . . and I defy anyone to say that and chew gum at the same time."

On at least one occasion, Ford gained a measure of revenge for Lyndon Johnson's jokes at his expense. Said Ford, "Henry Clay always said he'd rather be right than president. Now President Johnson has proved it really is a choice."

The first American president to visit Japan, Ford was the subject of an unintentional photo opportunity, thanks to a pair of diplomatic striped pants that barely reached the top of his socks. Returning to Washington, he summoned speechwriter Bob Orben to the Oval Office and said, "Did you see that picture?"

Orben professed ignorance. "What picture?" he asked Ford, who simply smiled and said, "You know what picture. We've got to have some fun with that." And so they did. As it turned out, that very evening the president was scheduled to address a Boy Scout banquet in Washington. This is how he opened his speech:

> They say once a Scout, always a Scout, and I can tell you from my own experience that it is true. After all these years I still love the outdoors. I still know how to cook for myself, at least breakfast. And as anyone who saw those pictures of me in Japan will know, on occasion I still go around in short pants.

A true child of Capitol Hill, Ford knew exactly how to get a message communicated to his former colleagues. In the winter of 1975, lawmakers were about to pass a $28-billion tax cut sought by Ford—without enacting the necessary budget cuts to pay for it. Ford instructed his congressional liaison to call up the parliamentarian of Congress and ask what the rules were for calling that august body back to Washington for a special session during the Christmas recess.

"Now," said Ford, "make sure that you tell the parliamentarian that I want to keep this an absolute secret. That will get the word around the Hill faster than Western Union."

Which is exactly what happened. Ford's threat got circulated, and Congress passed a compromise budget before adjourning.

White House photographer David Kennerly was forever puncturing Washington pomposity. When the president slipped and tumbled down an airplane stairway, Kennerly interrupted his picture-taking long enough to say, "So nice you could drop in."

In 1975 the Ford White House was mired in gloom, as U.S. involvement in South Vietnam came to a humiliating conclusion. Kennerly appeared in the office of the National Security Council and declared, "Well, I have good news and bad news. The good news is the Vietnam War is over. The bad news is we lost."

During the 1976 campaign, Ford's pardon of Nixon refused to go away. Journalist Fred Barnes got up at a press conference and said, "Mr. President, two or three times today you talked about your 'predecessor,' and once you referred to 'Lyndon Johnson's successor.' Are you trying to avoid saying the name Richard M. Nixon?"

"Yes," said Ford.

Ford's campaign against Jimmy Carter was enlivened by the president's misstatement during a crucial debate concerning Soviet domination of Poland. Following his narrow defeat, there was much speculation about Ford's post–White House career. Some thought he might become a professor at the University of Michigan. He was considering this, said Ford, before adding, "I'm not going to teach Eastern European history, however."

At the time of the November 1997 dedication of the Bush Presidential Library at Texas A&M, Ford said that he and President Bush had much in common. "To begin with, each of us married above himself, thereby demonstrating that behind every great woman is a man wondering what she ever saw in him." Ford also liked to remind people that both he and Bush had occasionally, if unfairly, been accused of mangling the English language, and of believing that syntax is something you slap on a bottle of bourbon. In the wake of the recent discovery of secret White House recordings by previous administrations, Ford reminded listeners, "There aren't any Ford or Bush tapes. But even if there were, you probably wouldn't understand what was on them."

#20 RUTHERFORD B. HAYES

At the age of eighteen, Hayes confided to his diary that "my level of fun is so great, and my perception of the ludicrous so quick, that I laugh at everything witty, and say all I can to add to the general mirth." So far, so good. What followed was the mark of the politician in training. His humorous nature was "agreeable enough at times," said Hayes, "but the tendency to carry it to extremes is so great that I shall stop it entirely in future, if I can."

Most historians think he was successful in his resolve.

Writing to his sons, Hayes administered some very Victorian counsel: "Never do anything or say anything that you would be ashamed to confide to your mother."

Hayes wasn't always the cautious political suitor. "Fighting battles is like courting girls," he once asserted. "Those who make the most pretensions and are boldest usually win."

A true reformer, Hayes feared the emergence of economic injustice and class politics. "Abolish plutocracy if you would abolish poverty," he remarked.

Like most presidents, Hayes felt ill-used by the daily press. "I would honor the man who would give to his country a good newspaper," he once said.

Thanks to his disputed election over Democrat Samuel J. Tilden in 1876, Hayes's critics dubbed the president His Fraudulency. Yet Hayes quickly showed himself a man of principle, unwilling to defer to his own party's bosses in the Senate. Chief among these was the imperious boss of New York politics, Senator Roscoe Conkling, whose staunch opposition to civil service reform brought him into open conflict with the man he sneeringly called Granny Hayes. In the end, Hayes had the last laugh, defeating Conkling in the Senate and savoring his rival's humiliation at the hands of a former Rhode Island governor with whose wife Conkling had been carrying on an indiscreet affair.

Soon all Washington was abuzz with the story of Conkling's making his escape through a bedroom window, clutching his trousers, one step ahead of a gun-toting husband. "This exposure of Conkling's rottenness will do good in one direction," noted Hayes in his diary. "It will weaken his political power, which is bad and only bad." White House celebrations were inevitably muted, given the abstemious ways of the president and his wife, whose temperance crusade had earned her the nickname Lemonade Lucy. As news of Hayes's triumph over Conkling circulated, it was said, "The buttermilk flowed at the White House like water."

For months before leaving the White House, Hayes reminded visitors of a man about to be pardoned. "Out of a scrape," he kept chuckling, "out of a scrape."

Unlike many other presidents, Hayes counted the days until he was released from the presidency's burdens. He likened it to escaping from bondage. "I am glad to be a *freed man*," said Hayes.

#21 WILLIAM MCKINLEY

McKinley was a natural politician, highly popular with his colleagues. Among these was young James Garfield, who claimed that no one surpassed McKinley's skill in hitting the cuspidors that lined the walls of the House restaurant.

In 1892, Republicans fearing defeat if the unpopular Benjamin Harrison was renominated looked to McKinley as an alternative. The shrewd Ohioan, however, had no desire to run in a Democratic year. Having safely seen Harrison to a first-ballot victory at his party's convention, an exhausted McKinley returned to his hotel. Accompanying him were a friendly newspaperman and the industrialist Mark Hanna, soon to win immortality of sorts as McKinley's successful campaign manager. Amid the bruising heat, the men threw off their outer clothes, then stretched out on the sofa and beds. For a while, the only sound was that of ice cubes tinkling in their glasses. At last Hanna broke the stillness and said, "My God, William, that was a damned close squeak."

Eighteen ninety-six was a no-holds-barred contest between William Jennings Bryan, the scourge of Wall Street, and McKinley, the high-tariff man. Like Ronald Reagan almost a century later, McKinley had a genius for simplifying the complex. Learned professors and economic experts might debate the arcane intricacies of the gold standard. He had his own way of framing the issue: "Good money never made times hard." It was one of the more effective slogans in American political history.

Theodore Roosevelt and other reform-minded Republicans joined the thousands of pilgrims making the trip to McKinley's home in Canton, Ohio, where supporters wearing gold-colored neckties were led by bands playing the campaign anthem, "The Honest Little Dollar's Come to Stay." TR's acerbic friend John Hay was among those paying court to "the Majah." Hay saw something that eluded more conventional observers. "I was more struck than ever with his mask," noted Hay. "It is a genuine Italian ecclesiastical face of the fifteenth century. And there are idiots who think Mark Hanna will run him!"

Part cynic, part sophisticate, John Hay had a field day with McKinley's earnest opponent, the thirty-six-year-old congressman from Nebraska and Free Silver advocate, William Jennings Bryan. "The Boy Orator makes only one speech—but he makes it twice a day," wrote Hay. "There is no fun in it. He simply reiterates the unquestioned truths that every man who has a clean shirt is a thief and ought to be hanged; that there is no goodness or wisdom except among the illiterate and criminal classes; that gold is vile; that silver is lovely and holy . . . he has succeeded in scaring the Goldbugs out of their five wits."

McKinley possessed a quiet irony mixed with shrewdness. For example, as congressional pressure built for a more aggressive policy toward Spain, the president refused to be hurried. "Impatience is not patriotism," he observed. On another occasion, when his personal secretary handed McKinley a fund-raising letter from a church in his hometown of Canton, Ohio, McKinley returned it with the notation, "Call that to my attention when I feel richer than now."

As undersecretary of the navy, the bellicose Theodore Roosevelt could barely conceal his eagerness for war with Spain. Sometimes this caused him to be indiscreet, as when he said of the peace-loving President McKinley, "He has all the backbone of a chocolate éclair." The *Chicago Tribune* saw it differently. "If this man, the first President of the new century, has no backbone, then we are invertebrate animals," said the paper.

Paperwork has always been the bane of presidents, but rarely has it bothered anyone as much as McKinley, who was forced to personally sign army and navy commissions during the Spanish-American War. His desk was covered with hundreds of the documents, each made of sheepskin and therefore impossible to blot.

At first McKinley went at his task cheerfully enough, humming a Methodist tune and clenching a cigar between his lips. After a while, the floor of his office all but disappeared under a snowfall of official paper. "Something ought to be done about this," McKinley grumbled. "Somebody else ought to be able to sign these."

On being told that congressmen were unhappy over a broken elevator in the White House, McKinley said, laughing, "Let them complain. It's too easy for them to get up here the way it is."

The Spanish-American War severely tested McKinley's sweet temper. When a politically inept adjutant general prematurely released news of several major appointments, he earned a rare presidential rebuke. "It's a good plan to call some people down now and then," McKinley explained afterward. "We all need to be called down once in a while."

Another fracas ensued when the same warrior showed up late for a White House dinner, then ascribed his tardiness to a slow watch.

"Lincoln once had an adjutant general who gave this same excuse," said McKinley. " 'Well,' said Mr. Lincoln, 'either you must get a new watch or I must get a new adjutant general.' "

McKinley labored far harder than his genial image suggested. At the close of the Spanish-American War he summoned an army officer for a close interrogation about Cuban finances.

"You do a great deal of work over here," said the soldier, barely concealing his surprise.

"Oh, no!" McKinley replied. "We don't work any over here. We just sit around."

Beneath McKinley's bland exterior were hints of resentment against those of greater sophistication or wealth. "I would rather have my political economy founded upon the everyday experience of the puddler or the potter than the learning of the professor," he remarked. At the same time, his quiet humor stood in marked contrast to the savage wit, as jagged as broken glass, employed by his chief rival in the GOP, Speaker of the House Tom Reed. "Everybody enjoys Reed's sarcastic comments," McKinley noted, "except the fellow who is the subject of his satire."

There has never been anyone in American politics quite like Thomas Brackett Reed, a physical and intellectual giant who was never deadlier than in the cut and thrust of debate. While McKinley made friends every time he opened his mouth, Reed made points—and friends are much more helpful in gaining the presidency. For instance, when a long-winded orator from Illinois concluded one turgid address by waving his arms and proclaiming, "like the great commoner from Kentucky, Henry Clay, I would rather be right than be president," Speaker Reed was more than prepared.

"The gentleman from Illinois need not be alarmed," said Reed. "He will never be either."

McKinley offered some "fatherly advice" to a young legislator. "No matter how long you stay in Congress," he said, "devote your time to killing vicious legislation rather than in preparing and introducing bills just to get your name in the newspapers. You will not reach the headlines that way, you will not attract so much attention as if you were 'shelling the woods' all the time, but you will render a vast service to the people and always be justified by a vindicating conscience."

To William Allen White, McKinley seemed anything but engaging. "He walked among men a bronze statue," sneered the Kansas editor, "for thirty years determinedly looking for his pedestal."

McKinley agonized over annexing the Philippines and other foreign territories won in the Spanish-American War. What he called "benevolent assimilation" struck the novelist Henry James as something quite different. As James summed up McKinley's position, "We're here for your own good, therefore unconditionally surrender to our tender mercies, or we'll blow you into kingdom come."

By nature a kindly man, McKinley nursed no grievance, harbored no grudges. To one political associate he offered shrewd advice: "Never keep books in politics." At the same time, the president was sensitive as a tuning fork to shifts in public opinion. One wag said that McKinley's ear was so close to the ground that it was full of grasshoppers.

#22 JIMMY CARTER

"I think probably politicians are about half ego and half humility," said candidate Carter in 1975. "I think I have my share of both of them."

In May 1977, President Carter delivered a commencement address at the University of Notre Dame. He began by comparing how the graduates must feel on going out into the world, and how he felt as a new president. "I was sitting on the Truman Balcony the other night with my good friend Charles Kirbo, who told me about a man who was arrested and taken into court for being drunk and for setting a bed on fire. When the judge asked him how he pled, he said, 'Not guilty.' He said, 'I was drunk but the bed was on fire when I got in it.'"

President Carter encouraged his staff to communicate clearly with the American people. Nonetheless, one White House letter included this sentence: "Based on my personal knowledge of the issue and of its inherent difficulties, I would be less than forthcoming if I failed to caution you not to be unduly optimistic about a favorable outcome."

Another Carter White House letter contained this memorable opening: "Thank you for taking the time to write President Carter, sharing with him the contents of your lengthy conversation with your dog, Spot."

Carter wasn't above needling his own brother, the irrepressible Billy. According to the president, "I've tried to involve Billy in the government. I was going to put the CIA and the FBI together, but Billy said he wouldn't head an agency that he couldn't spell."

Carter's sharp tongue did not desert him on a visit to Egypt. Informed by a guide that the Great Pyramid of Giza was built in just twenty years, the president replied, "I'm surprised that a government organization could do it that quickly."

Carter could be especially rough on the press. He actually began one public appearance with the words "I'm not going to say anything terribly important tonight, so you can all put away your crayons."

"We're all fuzzy on the issues," Carter once acknowledged. "That's proven by the fact that we did get elected. The advantage of being a presidential candidate is that you have a much broader range of issues on which to be fuzzy."

The combination of double-digit inflation, runaway interest rates, soaring gasoline prices, and American hostages in Iran sent Carter's public-opinion ratings into the basement. Greeted by loud, and unusual, applause at an event outside Washington, the president deadpanned, "It really is a pleasure to see people waving at me with all five fingers."

Stick-in-the-Mud

***

#23 ULYSSES GRANT

Grant is the great American puzzle. In the words of his friend William Tecumseh Sherman, his "whole character was a mystery even to himself." Brilliant if brutal as a military strategist, Grant seemed out of his depth in the political arena. Perhaps it was no accident that the president's favorite book was Mark Twain's *Innocents Abroad.* Grant's years in the White House were tinged by scandal; charity, apparently, began at home. Grant's own brother-in-law conspired with Wall Street speculators led by Jim Fisk—said to be "first in war, first in peace, and first in the pockets of his countrymen"—to corner the gold market.

When the bubble burst, so did Grant's reputation. Meanwhile, the plainspoken soldier turned politician barely disguised his contempt for the strutting peacocks of Capitol Hill. Displaying a caustic wit for which he was little credited, Grant called the imperious Senator Charles Sumner "a narrow head . . . his eyes are so close together he can peek through a gimlet hole without blinking." Informed that Sumner took issue with the Bible, Grant said, "That's because he did not write it."

Grant's 1872 opponent, Horace Greeley, was predictably critical. "Grant could afford to be a deaf and dumb candidate," said Greeley, "but the country can't afford to elect a deaf and dumb president."

Even praise from Grant's friends had a certain equivocation to it. General William Tecumseh Sherman said it best: "Grant stood by me when I was crazy, and I stood by him when he was drunk, and now we stand by each other."

Grant's overwhelming reelection in 1872 made him even more than usually contemptuous of reformers in his own party who had joined with Democrats in opposing him. The noise raised by Republican reformers, Grant told Congressman James Garfield, called to mind the first time he had ever heard prairie wolves. When the ruckus first greeted his ears, he concluded there had to be at least a hundred of them, but on drawing closer he discovered but two lonely wolves barking at each other.

In 1872, Susan B. Anthony scandalized her neighbors in upstate New York by violating suffrage laws that restricted voting to men only. "Well, I have gone and done it," she boasted to a friend. "Positively voted the Republican ticket–straight." (This was before the gender gap.) This wasn't as great a tribute to President Grant as it might appear–Horace Greeley, Grant's opponent in that year's presidential race, had done nothing to bolster his chances by informing Ms. Anthony that "the best women I know do not want to vote."

Nor was the champion of equal rights for women satisfied when Grant went on to appoint five thousand members of her sex to serve as postmasters. "Isn't that enough?" the president asked Anthony. Far from it, she answered. What she sought was "justice, not favors."

Grant was dismissive of the erudite James Garfield and his friends, whom he called a bunch of "damned literary fellows."

Grant, whose problems with the bottle were notorious, might have been anticipating America's later experiment with Prohibition when he wrote that he knew of no method "to secure the repeal of bad or obnoxious laws so effective as their stringent execution."

As the scandals of his administration piled up around Grant, James Garfield professed astonishment over the president's attitude. "His imperturbability is amazing," said Garfield. "I am in doubt whether to call it greatness or stupidity."

To Harry Truman, Grant may have been a great soldier. And in the White House? "The worst president in our history," declared the man from Missouri.

After leaving the White House in 1877, Grant embarked on an around-the-world tour. He observed that Venice would be a very fine city indeed if only someone had the sense to drain the canals. This was on a par with his earlier remark, when invited to show his musical appreciation, that he knew only two tunes: one was "Yankee Doodle" and the other wasn't.

A political scientist before he was a president, Woodrow Wilson could not resist passing judgment on Grant. "He combined great gifts with great mediocrity," said Wilson. We don't know what Grant thought of Wilson.

Cynical but amusing, Henry Adams was the ultimate misanthrope. For most Americans, the future is their friend. Not Adams. "A study of the presidency from Washington to Grant," he wrote, "is sufficient to disprove Darwin."

#24 JAMES MONROE

Writing to Thomas Jefferson, Monroe the proud father revealed, "Mrs. Monroe hath added a daughter to our society who, tho' noisy, contributes greatly to its amusement."

As a young man about to embark upon a hazardous frontier journey, Monroe offered friends reassurances. "It is possible I may lose my scalp from the temper of the Indians," he wrote, "but if either a little fighting or a great deal of running will save it, I shall escape safe."

As a dashing war veteran, and a promising politician, the youthful Monroe had more than his share of feminine admirers. "Poor Colonel Monroe!" wrote one. "I fear his love did not meet with a return, but we were blind and not acquainted with one half his perfections of person and mind, they were summed up to me this day and amounted to eight which includes every perfection that a female could wish or man envy. He is a member of

Congress, rich, young, sensible, well read, *lively,* and *handsome.* I forget the other accomplishment."

In February 1810, Monroe wrote to his friend William Short, urging him to move to the Charlottesville area, where he could be part of what Jefferson called "a society to our taste."

"You expressed a desire to sell your land near me," said Monroe. "Can you not come and reside on it? If you cannot prevail on a Lady from one of our great cities to bury herself there with you, one might be found in the neighborhood, of merit and worth, to whom the solitude would not be irksome. If you ever intend to make such an arrangement, you ought not to postpone it much longer. I am now 51 years of age; you are I presume not more than 10 years younger. In 1795 when we were in Paris together you were about 5 years younger. In 1775 when we were at College the difference between us was still less. I hope you will take this affair into consideration, and decide in favor of my counsel, and come and establish yourself near me ere long."

Monroe's appointment of John Quincy Adams as secretary of state pleased Thomas Jefferson, who knew both men. "They were made for each other," said the ex-president. "Adams has a pointed pen; Monroe has judgment enough for both and firmness enough to have his judgment control."

Having held more offices than any other president, Monroe was thoroughly steeped in Washington byways. Near the end of a lengthy White House reception, a friend asked the president if he felt tired. "Oh, no," Monroe answered. "A little flattery will support a man through great fatigue."

Like George Washington, Monroe traveled extensively throughout the young republic, to see and be seen. His 1817 visit to Haverhill, Massachusetts, coincided with that of a touring circus. Young John Greenleaf Whittier, who would grow up to become a famous poet, was prohibited by his strict Quaker parents from seeing either the president or the traveling show of wild animals. Walking into town the next day, the nine-year-old Whittier encountered an impression left in the dusty road by an elephant's foot. Naturally, the boy assumed it to be the imprint of the president of the United States. Whittier returned home, happily convinced that he had seen at least the footprint of the greatest man on earth.

Not everyone was so impressed by Monroe. Aaron Burr denounced the president as "naturally dull and stupid; extremely illiterate; indecisive to a degree that would be incredible to one who did not know him . . . of course, hypocritical; he has no opinion on any subject and will always be under the government of the worst men." And you thought modern presidents had it rough.

Monroe's administration was famously dubbed the Era of Good Feelings. Perhaps, but among his ambitious cabinet, jockeying for the succession tested even Monroe's amiability. At one point Secretary of the Treasury William Crawford—characterized by Secretary of State John Quincy Adams as "a worm preying upon the vitals of the administration"—rudely challenged the president over federal patronage. Monroe raised his voice. Crawford raised his cane, as if to strike the elderly chief executive.

"You damned infernal old scoundrel," cried Crawford.

Seizing a pair of fireplace tongs in self-defense, Monroe ordered the secretary of the treasury out of the White House. So much for good feelings.

In a world still hostile toward popular government, Monroe earned respect for the United States by standing on ceremony. Even within the refined precincts of the White House, however, the old man was sometimes called on to play peacemaker. One evening over dinner the British minister noticed that every time he made a remark, the ambassador of France bit his thumb.

"Do you bite your thumb at me, sir?" demanded the Englishman.

"I do!" shot back his Gallic counterpart.

With that, the two diplomats put down their dinnerware and rushed out. They were about to fight a duel with swords in the vestibule of the president's house when Monroe showed up, preventing bloodshed by ordering carriages for both men.

In 1820, Monroe won overwhelming reelection. In fact, he received every electoral vote but one—that withheld by a stubborn New Hampshire elector named William Plumber, who insisted on casting it for John Quincy Adams—in part to advertise Adams's claims for 1824, but also to deny the last Virginia president the unanimous acclaim accorded the first. In modern parlance, Plumber might well have said to President Monroe, "I knew George Washington. George Washington was my friend. And you're no George Washington."

During the 1824 campaign, Monroe wrote briskly to his attorney general, William Wirt. "I hope that you and your family are in good health. It will give me pleasure to see you here," said the president, "you not being a candidate for a certain office."

#25 Richard Nixon

In May 1952, then-Senator Nixon appeared before the annual fund-raising dinner of the New York State Republican Party. He did not know it at the time, but his appearance was a job interview, arranged by Governor Thomas E. Dewey, the kingmaker behind General Dwight Eisenhower's presidential campaign. Dewey was in the market for a vice president, and Nixon advanced his prospects with a powerful speech, delivered without notes, asserting the need for Republicans to attract millions of Democratic and independent voters if they were to have any hope of victory in November.

Concluding his remarks, Nixon returned to his seat at the dais next to Dewey. The dapper governor of New York stamped out a cigarette and gave his guest some advice. "Make me a promise," Dewey told Nixon. "Don't get fat, don't lose your zeal, and you can be president someday."

The ancient notion of a balanced ticket rests upon the even more ancient belief that opposites attract. Yet it is just as likely that opposites will remain opposites, and for good reason. Certainly, the Eisenhower-Nixon marriage had its rocky moments. After the GOP convention in Chicago, Ike the outdoorsman invited his understudy to join him on a fishing trip in Colorado. There he instructed Nixon in the fine art of trout casting. On his first three attempts, Nixon hooked a tree limb. The fourth time he caught Eisenhower's shirt. So much for balance.

In September 1955, President Eisenhower suffered a heart attack while visiting his in-laws in Denver. On learning the news, Nixon summoned his old friend Bill Rogers, then acting attorney general in the Eisenhower cabinet. Neither man had any idea what, if any, legal position the vice president occupied under such circumstances. An embarrassed Rogers began looking for a copy of the Constitution. Unable to find one in his son's school-books, he picked up the phone to call his office at the Justice Department.

"For God's sake, don't do that," Nixon told him. "If it ever gets out that the vice president and the attorney general don't know what the Constitution says, we'd look like a couple of complete idiots."

Following his narrow loss to John F. Kennedy in the 1960 election, it couldn't have been easy for Nixon to wring laughter from the situation. Nevertheless, he described himself as "a dropout from the Electoral College," who had unintentionally "flunked debating."

In the early 1960s, Nixon was out of office and practicing law in New York. He also worked hard at mending fences, including some thought to be irreparable. At a Gridiron Dinner, Nixon even sought out his old political enemy Harry Truman and bought him a bourbon and water. When it came his turn to speak, Nixon recounted the incident for his audience, adding that love was really bursting out all over when Harry Truman accepted a drink from Richard Nixon without having it tested first.

In the spring of 1964, then private citizen Richard Nixon commented on that year's race for the presidency, which was shaping up to be a LBJ landslide, telling one audience, "[You] should see some of my mail. I received a letter the other day which said, "The Republicans should nominate you. They're going to lose anyway. Why not choose an expert in losing?"

An aggressive campaigner, Nixon made no apologies for his tactics on the stump. "You don't win campaigns with a diet of dishwater and milk toast," he said.

One Sunday during the 1968 campaign, Nixon went to hear an evangelist speak on the topic "The Gospel in a Revolutionary Age." The candidate was deeply moved by this appeal for personal and national repentance. What's more, Nixon had a highly personal reason to appreciate the sermon. As he explained it, "The press go with me everywhere, and that was a great message for them to hear."

On another occasion, Nixon was attending a Billy Graham crusade in Knoxville, Tennessee, only to be embarrassed by an empty wallet when the offering plate was passed. Somehow Billy managed to slip the president all the cash in his own pocket. Afterward, Graham received a letter on White House stationery revealing an unusual streak of Nixonian whimsy.

"A number of Presidents have looked to you for spiritual sustenance over the years, but I suspect I was the first to hit you for a loan . . . while deficit financing can be useful in a pinch, the time always comes when the deficit must be funded. In keeping with my concern for fiscal responsibility, I'm hereby repaying your loan."

Nixon's British biographer Jonathan Aitkin recalled how, at their final meeting, he apologized in advance for a book that was bound to fall short of being definitive. The president asked Aitkin to explain. "I mean," said Aitkin, "I have come to the conclusion that you are too complicated a character to be captured accurately by the pen of a mortal writer."

"Aha," Nixon chuckled, "now I know you are really getting somewhere."

President Nixon and Vice President Agnew brought down the house at the 1970 Gridiron Dinner with a surprise piano duet. But the funniest line of the night was probably that of Soviet ambassador Dobrynin, who, upon seeing Nixon and Agnew both leave the room to prepare for their surprise, turned to Secretary of State Bill Rogers and asked, "Is it the custom in your country when the president goes to the men's room, the vice president has to accompany him?"

The veteran journalist Lou Cannon recalls one of the unintentional funniest lines ever uttered in the White House. It came from Ron Ziegler, Nixon's embattled press secretary, who was delivering a year-end review during an especially bleak period for the administration. As Ziegler put it, "We had a good year, except for Watergate."

#26 JOHN TYLER

When Charles Dickens visited the United States in 1842, he was repelled by the American custom of expectorating. Dickens portrayed for his readers the blizzard of spittle enveloping trains on parallel tracks. Nor was the author any more impressed by John Tyler's Washington.

"Take the worst parts of the City Road and Pentonville," wrote Dickens, "put green blinds outside all the private houses, with a red curtain and a white one in every window; pile up all the roads; plant a great deal of coarse turf where it ought *not* to be; erect three handsome buildings in stone and marble, anywhere, but the more entirely out of everybody's way, the better; call one the Post Office, one the Patent Office, and one the Treasury; make it scorching hot in the morning, and freezing cold in the afternoon, with an occasional tornado of wind and dust; leave a brickfield with the bricks, in all central places where a street may naturally be expected; and that's Washington."

The White House reminded Dickens of an English clubhouse, albeit one lacking doorman or butler. What the house *did* teem with were suspicious Yankees eyeing whatever might be portable, "as if to make quite sure that the President (who was far from popular) had not made away with any of the furniture, or sold the fixtures for his private benefit." Dickens found Tyler sitting at a table covered with papers. The chief magistrate looked both worn and anxious, "and well he might; being at war with everybody—but the expression of his face was mild and pleasant, and his manner was remarkably unaffected, gentlemanly, and agreeable."

"Popularity, I have always thought, may aptly be compared to a coquette," mused Tyler. "The more you woo her, the more apt is she to elude your embrace."

In 1844, President Tyler didn't hesitate to use federal employees to advance his slender political prospects. That postmasters should be directed to promote a Tyler campaign biography was hardly surprising, given the spoils system first instilled by Andrew Jackson. What *was* blatant, even by the standards of the day, was the accompanying note drawn up by the president's secretary. "Prompt attention and a liberal subscription will render your services still more useful," it read, above the signature of John Tyler Jr.

Harry Truman required few words to sum up Tyler: "He was a contrary old son of a bitch."

Humorist Richard Armour provided another assessment of Tyler's historical significance. "He was the first vice president to become president through the death of a president," said Armour, "which was a good thing for him but a bad thing for Harrison."

Long before the end of his term, Tyler found himself disowned by the Whigs and superseded by the Democratic nominee for president, James K. Polk. Shortly before Tylor left Washington, a gala White House event was staged to bid farewell to the Tylers. Two thousand invitations had been sent out, and the mansion was lit by a thousand candles. "They cannot say now that I am a president without a party," said Tyler.

A former Democrat turned Whig turned independent, as an ex-president Tyler named his Virginia plantation Sherwood Forest—for that other famous outlaw of history whose intentions were good, notwithstanding what the authorities might think of him.

#27 ANDREW JACKSON

In a blatant effort to promote potential rivals out of the 1824 presidential contest, Secretary of State John Quincy Adams asked President Monroe if he had thought of appointing the fiery Jackson to a foreign diplomatic post—the farther from Washington, the better.

"Yes," Monroe replied, "but I'm afraid he would get us into a quarrel."

Jackson and his predecessor, John Quincy Adams, enjoyed—if that is the right word—one of the epic feuds in American political history. Adams called Jackson "incompetent both by his ignorancy and by the fury of his passions."

Far from the frontier ruffian of legend, Jackson managed to charm even chilly New Englanders when he visited the region in the summer of 1833. Harvard reluctantly invited the president to visit Cambridge and receive an honorary degree, leading to Adams's boycott of the ceremony. He could hardly believe, said Adams, that fair Harvard would disgrace herself "by conferring her highest literary honors upon a barbarian who could not write a sentence of grammar and could hardly spell his own name."

In the event, Jackson showed unwonted dignity amidst the formality of a Harvard commencement, most of which was transacted in Latin. According to legend, when it came his turn to speak, the old man rose gracefully from his seat, bowed to his audience, and declaimed, "Ipso facto. Tempus fugit. Sine qua non. E pluribus unum."

The occasion was marred only by Jackson's continuing ill health, which prompted concern everywhere but in the Adams household. Suspicious as ever, the former president accused Jackson of exploiting his poor health "like John Randolph, who for forty years was always dying."

The father of the spoils system ("to the victor belong the spoils"), Jackson told his colleagues, "If you have a job in your department that can't be done by a Democrat, then abolish the job."

On another occasion, Jackson defined the presidency as "a situation of dignified slavery."

Like other presidents, Jackson received numerous presents from admirers. Among these was a fourteen-hundred-pound cheese from upstate New York. A team of twenty-four gray horses drew a flag-draped wagon bearing the monster cheese on its journey to Washington, where it sat in the vestibule of the White House for almost two years. As Jackson's term neared its end, the president decided there was only one way to get rid of the gift. So he issued a public invitation for Washington's birthday, 1837.

In response, thousands showed up. "Mr. Van Buren was there to eat cheese," reported a local newspaper. "Mr. Webster was there to eat cheese; Mr. Woodbury, Colonel Benton, Mr. Dickerson," and countless others. "All you heard was cheese; all you smelled was cheese." Indeed, the atmosphere around the White House for half a mile was permeated with the aroma of cheese. There are worse smells that can emanate from the White House.

On his deathbed, Jackson was asked if he had any regrets. He did, said the old man: "That I didn't shoot Henry Clay and hang John C. Calhoun."

Out of earshot, one onlooker around Jackson's deathbed asked another, "Do you think the general will go to heaven?"

"Well," he was told, "if he wants to go, who is going to stop him?"

#28 CHESTER ARTHUR

Woodrow Wilson called Arthur "a nonentity with side whiskers."

A widower, Arthur frequently saw in the Washington newspapers his name linked with eligible women. He didn't like what he read. "Madame," he told one Nosy Parker, "I may be president of the United States, but my private life is nobody's damn business."

No workaholic, Arthur registered a unique presidential complaint. "You have no idea how depressing and fatiguing it is," he said, "to live in the same house where you work."

Most mornings he arrived in his office about ten and left by four or five at the latest. As one White House clerk phrased it, "President Arthur never did today what he could put off until tomorrow." He once required a month to copy a condolence letter destined for a European court—a message already drafted by the State Department.

A man known to occasionally bend the elbow, Arthur nevertheless issued a stiff protest on being told that a prominent government official had been intoxicated. "No gentleman ever sees another gentleman drunk," insisted the president.

Estranged from his former protégé, the disgraced Roscoe Conkling hurled the ultimate insult at the new regime. "I have but one annoyance with the administration of President Arthur,"

said Conkling, "and that is, that in contrast with it, the administration of Hayes becomes respectable, if not heroic."

Arthur, a true epicurean, served eight varieties of wines with his fourteen-course dinners. The only thing Arthur loved better than food was clothing: the most stylish president before John Kennedy, Arthur was rumored to try on twenty pairs of trousers before finding just the right garment. When Arthur failed to win renomination in 1884, the acid-tongued Uncle Joe Cannon declared that the president "was defeated by his trousers."

Defeated for renomination in 1884, privately notified by his doctors that he was dying of kidney disease, Arthur left Washington as quietly as he had come, saying, "There doesn't seem to be anything else for an ex-president to do but go into the country and raise big pumpkins."

#29 JOHN QUINCY ADAMS

Almost from birth, Adams was reminded that not only his family's but his country's hopes rested upon him. From his strong-willed mother, he heard endless sermonizing about the need for self-control. "I never knew a man of great talents much given to laughter," said Abigail. "My own ideas of pleasure consist in tranquillity."

Like his father, John Quincy recoiled from party politics. In truth, he was a party of one. "I would sooner turn scavenger and earn my living by cleaning away the filth of the streets than plunge into this bottomless filth of faction."

At a public dinner given in Henry Clay's honor, the congenial Clay annoyed Adams by playing to the crowd. "It is a convenient practice," grumbled the starchy New Englander, "for men who wish to keep themselves forever in the public eye . . . a triple alliance of flattery, vanity, and egotism." In 1824, Clay, himself a presidential also-ran, held the trump card in the closely contested presidential race between Adams and Andrew Jackson. The final selection would fall to the House of Representatives, where Clay wielded immense influence. Naturally, he reveled in the suspense this created.

At a Washington party, Clay observed Adams and Jackson in uncomfortable proximity, separated by nothing more than a vacant chair. Deciding to have a little fun at their expense, Clay rose from his own seat, walked across the room, and plopped himself down between the would-be presidents.

"Well, gentlemen, since you are both so near the chair, but neither can occupy it, I will slip into it between you, and take it myself!" Much laughter followed, in which neither Adams nor Jackson joined.

Adams possessed a distinguished name, a remarkable résumé, and a brilliant mind keenly attuned to the problems and possibilities faced by young America. On the other hand, he may have been the most undiplomatic of diplomats. One English counterpart who had the misfortune to sit across from Adams at a negotiating table called him "a bulldog among spaniels." In later years, Ralph Waldo Emerson portrayed Adams as a bruiser who never missed a good fight and didn't hesitate to start one. "He is an old roué," said Emerson, "who cannot live on slops, but must have sulfuric acid in his tea."

One contemporary remarked of Adams that he had "an instinct for the jugular and the carotid arteries as unerring as that of any carnivorous animal."

Harry Truman once wrote, "The single really interesting thing about Adams, I'm afraid, is that he was the only son of a president in our history to become president himself."

By nature suspicious, Adams could not have been the easiest of men with whom to do business. At one point, he nearly came to blows with the British minister to the United States over the mouth of the Columbia River. The British diplomat protested some remarks in Congress questioning his country's claims to the region. Adams just as hotly resented foreign intrusion into his own country's domestic affairs. It was, he said, as if the American minister in London were to challenge a parliamentary inquiry about the Shetland Islands.

At this, the royal representative lost his temper and asked, "Have *you* any claim to the Shetland Islands?"

"Have *you* any claim to the mouth of the Columbia River?" retorted Adams.

"Do you not *know* that we have a claim?"

Actually, said Adams, the full extent of British claims was quite beyond his knowledge. "You claim India, you claim Africa, you claim—"

At this point the Englishman interrupted sarcastically, "Perhaps a piece of the moon?"

"No," said Adams, "I have not heard that you claim *exclusively* any part of the moon; but there is not a spot on *this* inhabitable globe that I affirm you do not claim."

JQA in his diary: "I am a man of reserved, cold, austere, and forbidding manners: my political adversaries say, a gloomy misanthropist, and my personal enemies, an unsocial savage."

The Adamses had been bred to see themselves as a special breed, selfless, self-sacrificing–and unappreciated. Said the first lady, "Our tastes, our tempers, our habits, vary so much from those of the herd that we can never be beloved or admired, but we may and must be respected–unless we forget the respect we owe ourselves."

Adams never forgave Thomas Jefferson for his treatment of Adams's father. Adams called the Virginian "a rare mixture of infidel philosophy and epicurean morals, of burning ambition and of stoical self-control, of deep duplicity and of generous sensibility."

You just knew that JQA would have something bitter to say about the press. Journalists, he once declared, "are a sort of assassin who sit with loaded blunderbusses at the corners of streets and fire them off for hire or for sport at any passenger they select."

No one knew Adams better than his long-suffering wife, Louisa. "He is a man with whom you cannot temporize," Mrs. Adams told her son Charles. "The little attentions which are mere commonplaces in this world are utterly lost upon a man who thinks it a great deal of offense to be asked to change his coat or to put on a clean shirt."

As James Monroe prepared to hand off the baton in 1824, he found not one or two, but five hands grasping for the prize. Three belonged to members of his own cabinet. One evening, half of official Washington crowded into Secretary Adams's home on F Street for a ball in honor of General Jackson on the anniversary of his triumph at the Battle of New Orleans. As one waggish guest put it:

> Belles and matrons, maids and madams,
> all are gone to Mrs. Adams.

To a friend who urged Adams to take a more active part in the campaign, the stiff Yankee replied with a quote from MacBeth: "If chance will have me king, why, chance may crown me, without my stir."

"This won't do," Adams's friend remarked to Mrs. Adams. "Kings are made by politicians and newspapers; and the man who sits down waiting to be crowned, whether by chance or just right, will go bareheaded all his life."

Having at last reached the top of the greasy pole, Adams spent a miserable four years in the White House. Discarding the cautious approach of his predecessor, he urged Congress to adopt a breathtaking program of federally funded roads and canals, scientific expeditions—even a national astronomical observatory. Adams also wanted to establish a naval academy, prompting Senator William Smith of South Carolina to remind him that neither Julius Caesar nor Lord Nelson had attended a naval academy. Indeed, claimed Smith, such an institution would only lead to what another representative called "degeneracy and corruption of the public morality."

In the White House, Louisa became a confirmed chocoholic, lying on a divan and writing lengthy letters extolling the healing qualities of fudge. Perhaps, being married to the sourest man in Washington, she took her pleasures where she could find them.

In *Profiles in Courage,* John F. Kennedy recounted a charged confrontation between Adams and a politically minded preacher of advanced years and questionable politics. Offended by the minister's manner, Adams told him "that in consideration of his age, I should only remark that he had one lesson yet to learn— *Christian charity.*"

The high-minded Adams refused to take vengeance on his political enemies. In practical terms this meant leaving most of them in office, where they worked overtime to undermine his reelection prospects. At one 1827 dinner, a toast was proposed to the president: "May he strike confusion through his foes!"

"As he has already done to his friends!" chimed in Daniel Webster.

I have a soft spot in my heart for Webster. John C. Calhoun said that Webster was the most qualified man in the country to fill the executive office, before adding that, of course, "he is too great a man ever to be made president."

Following the death of Adams, Webster struck most observers as the greatest of American statesmen. This view was not universally held. On hearing one admirer declare that "nobody was so wise as Webster looked," a Southern senator replied caustically, "Not even Webster himself!"

The election of 1828 was one of the most intense—and scurrilous—in American history. Among other things, President Adams was accused of profaning the Sabbath by traveling openly through Rhode Island and Massachusetts on the Lord's Day. He was also labeled a monarchist, an aristocrat, and for good measure, a pimp for the czar of Russia. Worst of all, the editor of one Pennsylvania newspaper denounced Adams for his purchase of a billiard table—"an instrument used by genteel and fashionable gamblers in high life to play, and sport their money and time . . . what sign was it, to see the *President of the United States* indulging either his taste for gentility, or for gambling, in expending the money, which is taken from the pockets of the people, in the purchase of *Tables* and *Balls, which Can be used for no purpose but for gambling.*"

It was Adams's custom to rise each morning before the sun, read a chapter of the Bible, and work on his vast correspondence. For years he complained that official duties deprived him of his old friends Cicero and Tacitus. Meanwhile, the old man nagged and bullied his three sons, driving them to meet his perfectionist standards.

"One hour of the morning lamp is better than three of the evening taper," he reminded anyone who would listen, before adding for emphasis, "Genius is the child of toil."

Adams's son Charles pointed out, quite accurately, that after rising at five, a vigorous round of exercise, and twelve hours of business, it was not uncommon for his father to nod off at the dinner table. In short, people who rise at an unnaturally early hour are conceited all morning, and sleepy the rest of the day.

#30 ANDREW JOHNSON

A true minimalist, Johnson summed up his approach to government as follows: "There are no good laws but such as repeal other laws."

Johnson also considered himself a friend to the middle class. "If the rabble were lopped off at one end and the aristocrats at the other, all would be well with the country."

Thaddeus Stevens was among the leaders of Johnson's impeachment. His characterization of the president was predictably biting. "You will remember that in Egypt He sent frogs, locusts, murrain, lice, and finally demanded the firstborn of every one of the oppressors," declared Stevens. In the nineteenth century, "We have been oppressed with taxes and debts, and He has sent us worse than lice, and has afflicted us with Andrew Johnson."

Like any good stump orator, Johnson occasionally struck off a memorable phrase. Once asked to define his philosophy, he put it this way: "The goal to strive for is a poor government but a rich people."

#31 JAMES MADISON

Daniel Webster was dismissive of the man his critics called Little Jimmy. "I do not like his looks any better than I like his administration," chortled Webster.

According to contemporary accounts, the nation's fourth president was a brilliant conversationalist, much addicted to punning and epigram. Maybe you had to be there; the written record, at least, provides little evidence to support the picture of a witty Madison. Still, the Sage of Montpelier had his moments. In speaking of his political rival John Jay, Madison credited him with two strong character traits—"suspicion and religious bigotry."

One of Madison's favorite wartime anecdotes concerned a French officer, as vain as he was delusional, in the American service. The Frenchman placed special value on the esteem in which he was held by the ladies. With this in mind, he urged a fellow officer to reveal what the world said of him.

"Be frank, now," he said, "tell me the truth." The friend hesitated, protesting that such matters were entirely too delicate to be repeated. This only increased the Frenchman's curiosity. He demanded a full report, and his friend finally relented. "The opinion of the world is divided; the men say you are an old woman, and the women say you are an old man."

When Congress adjourned from Philadelphia to Princeton to escape potential mutiny by disorderly soldiers demanding their back pay, someone said that the action was, after all, only *a flash in the pan*.

"Yes," Madison recorded the exchange, "but they *went off*."

Princeton was a small town, suddenly overcrowded with visiting lawmakers. Madison himself shared a small room with a colleague. So inadequate were the facilities that one congressman was obliged to lie in bed while the other was dressing. Thus were the members of Congress brought *into close quarters,* said Madison.

In his last years, Madison became celebrated as the Father of the Constitution, and one of the last of the Revolutionary generation of giants. He seemed amused by all this. "Having outlived so many of my contemporaries," he wrote at one point, "I ought not to forget that I may be thought to have outlived myself."

Madison probably got off his best line at the end. On the morning he died, he was approached by a solicitous member of the family who asked if anything was the matter.

"Nothing more than a change of mind," said Madison, who promptly expired.

#32 GROVER CLEVELAND

Present-day politicians have nothing on their Gilded Age counterparts when it comes to a scandalmongering press. Cleveland's manful acknowledgment of his illegitimate child in 1884 earned him denunciation from the *Cincinnati Penny Post* as "a boon companion to Buffalo harlots." At that, Cleveland got off relatively unscathed compared to a pair of Hoosier would-be presidents, Thomas Hendricks and Oliver Morton, who were introduced to readers of the *Chicago Tribune* with the following headline: "The Former's Name Untrammeled by Lust, the Latter's Reeking with Filth and Slime. A Few of the Hellish Liaisons of, and Attempted Seductions by, Indiana's Favorite Stud Horse."

By the way, Cleveland's opponent in that year's election, James G. Blaine, didn't exactly have a free ride. The man his admirers called the Plumed Knight was denounced by journalistic critics as Jingo Jim, the Continental Liar from the State of Maine. Mrs. Henry Adams was still more direct. To her, the Republican candidate was "the rat Blaine . . . the biggest, most infernal liar in Christendom."

It was said of Cleveland, "We love him for the enemies he has made." Cleveland himself appreciated the compliment. "A man is known by the company he keeps," said the candidate, "and also by the company from which he is kept out."

A reluctant politician by nature, in time even Cleveland succumbed to the lure of the presidency. "This office-seeking is a disease," he acknowledged. "It is even catching."

Said journalist Henry Stoddard of Cleveland, "As president, he could not dominate, and he did not know how to persuade." In truth, Cleveland had no gift for public relations. His staff only made things worse. "After the President had rubbed the skin off of visiting statesmen," wrote one observer, "[his secretary] Thurber came in the nature of strong fish brine to make his wounds smart." To make things worse, Cleveland didn't conceal his disdain for the press, with the result that reporters were left to gather information about his administration "much after the fashion in which highwaymen rob a stagecoach."

A bachelor at the time of his first election to the presidency in 1884, Cleveland invited his accomplished sister, Rose, to serve as his White House hostess. Miss Cleveland was a prominent lecturer on women's rights and a recognized literary scholar. She later confessed that she had passed the time during boring reception lines by silently conjugating Greek verbs.

Cleveland constantly argued with the Senate, although he got along reasonably well with its legislature counterpart on the other side of the Capitol. Retiring one night after the latest chapter in his ongoing war with the upper body, Cleveland fell into a fitful sleep. Not long after, a butler, hearing strange noises, awoke the president and said, "I think there are burglars in the house."

Replied Cleveland, "In the Senate, maybe, but not in the House."

#33 JAMES K. POLK

Polk was among those taking to the stump for Van Buren in 1836. John Quincy Adams was distinctly underwhelmed by Polk's oratory. It had "no wit, no literature, no point of argument," said Adams, "no gracefulness of delivery, no elegance of language, no philosophy, no pathos, no felicitous impromptus." At least Adams was bipartisan in his chastisements. "The remarkable character of this election," he observed in his diary, "is that all the candidates are at most third rate men whose pretensions rest not on high attainments or upon eminent services, but upon intrigue and political speculation."

Polk's stance as a man of the people was mocked by Mrs. John Quincy Adams, who noted that at Polk's 1832 wedding, not only the bride and groom but their political associates rode "in a very showy equipage with four fine-spirited horses." Was it possible that the new Mrs. Polk had been seduced by her husband's wealth? "The innocent country lass!!! Who will deny the charms of a carriage and four?"

A Puritan in politics as in life, Polk looked with disfavor on the scramble for position. "The passion for office among members of Congress is very great," he complained, "and greatly embarrasses the operations of the government. They create offices by their own votes and then seek to fill them themselves."

Once Polk entered the White House, he couldn't escape "the herd of lazy, worthless people who come to Washington for office, instead of going to work. . . . One of these office seekers placed his papers of recommendation" before the president, without bothering to specify any particular office to which he aspired. However, noted Polk, "He answered that he thought he would be a good hand at making treaties . . . and would like to be a minister abroad. This is about as reasonable as many other applications which are made to me."

Sarah Polk compensated for her husband's dour silences with a grace and charm that captivated everyone. Even political enemies. Sitting next to her one day at a White House dinner, Henry Clay turned to the first lady and remarked, "Madame, I must say that in all my travels, in all companies and among all parties, I have heard but one opinion of you. All agree in commending in the highest terms your excellent administration of the domestic affairs of the White House. But"—and here Clay looked over at Sarah's husband—"as for that young gentleman there, I cannot say as much."

"Indeed," said Mrs. Polk, "I am glad to hear that *my* administration is popular."

A good Presbyterian, Polk frowned upon dancing, horse races, the theater, and music on Sundays. Conscientious to a fault, the president has fared better with historians since than with his less rigorous contemporaries. Indeed, Sam Houston said the only problem with the Polks was that they drank too much water.

Polk may have presided over the American victory in the Mexican War, but most of the credit went to two Whig generals, Zachary Taylor and Winfield Scott. In time both men would seek the presidency; Scott especially was resentful of Polk. As the general put it, "I do not desire to place myself in the most perilous of all positions: a fire upon my rear from Washington, and the fire in front from the Mexicans."

To Abraham Lincoln, then a young Whig congressman opposed to the president's Mexican War policies, Polk appeared "a bewildered, confounded, and miserably perplexed man."

Polk broke with tradition by declaring in advance his refusal of a second term. Angered and overworked, he had few regrets on leaving Washington. In fact, he rejoiced at the prospect of turning his office over to another man. "I will soon cease to be a servant," said Polk, "and will become a sovereign."

The Joke's on Them

✯ ✯ ✯

#34 ZACHARY TAYLOR

On the eve of the 1848 election, the Whigs were desperately seeking a military hero in order to recapture the White House. Practically any soldier would do; convictions mattered far less than battlefield heroics. So when New York boss Thurlow Weed ran into Zachary Taylor's brother on a Hudson River steamboat, the timing seemed providential. Weed inquired as to the general's political principles. Taylor, it appeared, had none. He belonged to no party. He had seldom, if ever, cast a vote. To tell the truth, said Joseph Taylor, his brother Zachary possessed prejudices rather than principles—he liked Henry Clay, disliked Andrew Jackson, and refused to wear any imported clothing out of respect to American manufacturers.

"Your brother is to be our next president," Weed announced on the spot. Joseph Taylor was astonished. "When I tell you he is not as fit to be president as I am, you will see the absurdity of your suggestion."

The only fitness Weed was interested in was measured at the ballot box.

✯

Taylor had it about right when he wrote, "The idea that I should become President seems to me too visionary to require a serious answer. It has never entered my head, nor is it likely to enter the head of any other person."

Taylor was fortunate in his opponent, Lewis Cass of Michigan. As Horace Greeley put it, "The country does not deserve a visitation of that potbellied, mutton-headed cucumber Cass!" As for his own party's candidate, snapped the editor, "Old Zack is a good old soul, but don't know himself from a side of sole leather in the way of statesmanship."

Greeley was no more generous in assessing Taylor's cabinet, "a horrid mixture" akin to what a blind man would choose if turned loose among several hundred "would-be magnets of the Whig party, and ordered to touch and take."

The great educator Horace Mann called Taylor "a most simple-minded old man. He has the least show or pretension about him of any man I ever saw; talks as artlessly as a child about affairs of state, and does not seem to pretend to a knowledge of anything of which he is ignorant. He is a remarkable man in some respects; and it is remarkable that such a man should be president of the United States."

Even Taylor's diction came in for ridicule. In one message to Congress, he declared, "We are at peace with all of the world, and seek to maintain our cherished relations of amity with the rest of mankind."

On the Fourth of July, 1850, President Taylor attended a celebration on the Washington Monument grounds. Long-winded oratory and several hours in the broiling sun left him exhausted. Returning to the White House, the old man dined on some unwashed fruit, washed down with iced milk. Within days he was dead of cholera. He wasn't alone: one visitor wandering down Pennsylvania Avenue about this time was appalled to find a row of metallic coffins leaning against the wall of a building opposite Gadsby's Hotel—all because an enterprising undertaker expected to hit it rich during the sickly season.

Taylor's funeral was less than majestic. According to one congressman, "there was talking and drinking and any amount of fighting" during the ceremony. "This latter amusement I thought quite natural, for you know that old Zac was a great fighter."

Harry Truman was characteristically blunt on the subject of Taylor. "I can't be charitable and say that he failed to carry out his program," wrote Truman, "he didn't have any program to carry out."

#35 WARREN G. HARDING

On the eve of the 1920 Republican convention that nominated Harding, H. L. Mencken unleashed his fiercest sarcasm: "We move toward a lofty ideal. On some great and glorious day, the plain folks of the land will reach their heart's desire at last, and the White House will be adorned by a downright moron." To the Sage of Baltimore, Woodrow Wilson's successor was "a third-rate political wheelhorse, with the face of a moving-picture actor, the intelligence of a respectable agricultural-implements dealer, and the imagination of a lodge joiner."

At the same time, Mencken regarded Harding as the unintended consequence of Wilsonian idealism. After all the crusades of recent years, most Americans wanted nothing more than a rest. Or as Mencken put it, they are so "tired to death of intellectual charlatanry, they turn despairingly to honest imbecility."

Alice Roosevelt Longworth declared, "Harding was not a bad man. He was just a slob." His historical reputation has never recovered.

No one laughed harder than Harding in recalling his father's lament that "it's a good thing you weren't born a gal, Warren. You'd be in the family way all the time. You can't say no!"

Harding made no attempt to hide his intellectual deficiencies— or his political skills. "I don't know much about Americanism," he once said, "but it's a damned good word with which to carry an election."

When Harding's redoubtable wife, Florence, came downstairs on the first day of her husband's administration, she found White House servants drawing the window shades. Why were they doing that? she inquired. Because, she was told, people outside would crowd around the windows in hopes of getting a peek inside. Mrs. Harding ordered the shades be raised. "Let 'em look if they want to. It's their White House."

For all the jests inspired by his speechmaking, Harding could turn a phrase when he needed to. For example, on learning that he had unexpectedly won his party's nomination for president, he had the perfect explanation: "We drew a pair of deuces and filed."

Among those who voiced contempt for Harding's oratory was Wilson's son-in-law, William Gibbs McAdoo, who hoped to succeed to the presidency in 1920. "His speeches leave the impression of an army of pompous phrases moving over the landscape in search of an idea," remarked McAdoo. "Sometimes these meandering words would actually capture a struggling thought and bear it triumphantly a prisoner in their midst until it died of servitude and overwork."

For all his good intentions, Harding soon found himself swamped by the demands of office. "Jud," he asked his personal secretary, "you have a college education, haven't you? I don't know what to do or where to turn in this taxation matter. Somewhere there must be a book that tells all about it, where I could go to straighten it out in my mind. But I don't know where the book is, and maybe I couldn't read it if I found it! . . . My God, but this is a hell of a place for a man like me to be!"

Arthur S. Draper, foreign correspondent of the *New York Herald Tribune,* called on Harding after a lengthy tour of Europe, only to have the president decline his request for an interview. Instead Harding summoned his secretary-speechwriter, Judson Welliver. "I don't know anything about this European stuff," Harding told Draper. "You and Jud get together and he can tell me later; he handles these matters for me."

Worse lay ahead. In time, Harding learned of his betrayal by subordinates. "I can take care of my enemies all right," he blurted out to a friend, "but my goddamn friends, they're the ones keeping me walking the floor nights."

The first time comedian Will Rogers visited the Harding White House, it was the president who got off the best line. "This is the first time I ever got to see you," said Harding, "without paying for it."

One unfriendly biographer of Harding's helped perpetuate his image as a philanderer with a devastating couplet:

> His right eye was a good little eye,
> But his left eye loved to roam.

In the end, Harding was done in by the Ohio Gang, a boozy fraternity personified by one Jess Smith, the administration's court jester, who summed up his influence-peddling career in a favorite song of the period:

> My sister sells snow to the snowbirds
> My father makes bootlegger gin
> My mother, she takes in washing
> My God, how the money rolls in!

#36 MARTIN VAN BUREN

Ever the crafty politician, it was said of Van Buren that "he rode to his object with muffled oars."

A consummate diplomat, Van Buren worked his magic behind the scenes. As he put it, "Most men are not scolded out of their opinion."

To a critic in the business community Van Buren was nothing but "a sly, sneaking, adroit and practiced intriguer, who has risen from being the son of a grogshop keeper at Kinderhook, and subsequently a pettifogging attorney . . . by management and trickery alone."

When Andrew Jackson nominated his friend Van Buren to be ambassador to Great Britain, Vice President John C. Calhoun broke a Senate tie—and the nomination was rejected. A jubilant Calhoun told a colleague, "It will kill him, sir, kill him dead. He will never kick, sir, never kick."

Not only did Van Buren kick—in 1832 he replaced Calhoun as Jackson's vice president. Four years later he went on to occupy the White House himself.

Like her husband, Mrs. John Quincy Adams had a sharp tongue, and no reluctance to employ it when slashing political rivals. When Andrew Jackson gave way to the far less impressive Van Buren, Mrs. Adams couldn't resist marking the transition poetically:

> For the king of beasts we find no further use
> And the choice of the Nation now falls on a—goose.

Van Buren's foppish ways prompted ridicule from the frontiersman Davy Crockett. "When he enters the Senate chambers in the morning, he struts and swaggers like a crow in the gutter," Crockett said of then Vice President Van Buren. "He is laced up in corsets, such as women in a town wear, and, if possible, tighter than the best of them. It would be difficult to say from his personal appearance whether he was man or woman, but for his large red and gray whiskers. [He is] as distrustful, treacherous. . . . It is said that . . . he could laugh on one side of his face and cry on the other at one and the same time."

Cautious to a fault, Van Buren never let himself be pinned down to a position if he could avoid it. This became something of a joke among his colleagues, including a senator who bet a fellow lawmaker that he could trap the wily Van Buren into committing himself.

"Matt," said the senator, "it's been rumored that the sun rises in the east. Do you believe it?"

Van Buren wasn't buying and replied, "I understand that's the common acceptance, Senator, but as I never get up until after dawn, I can't really say."

Van Buren's first message to Congress, predictably, failed to impress John Quincy Adams. To Adams, the new president had simply delivered an earlier message from Jackson, "covered with a new coat of varnish."

Late in life, Van Buren declared the "two happiest days of my life were those of my entrance upon the presidency and my surrender of it." This did not prevent him from trying to recapture such happiness on more than one occasion.

Perpetually ambitious, Van Buren came by the title "the Red Fox of Kinderhook" naturally. Contemplating another try for the

White House in 1844, the former president needed to fan a draft. With this in mind, he handed a manuscript to young Sam Tilden, who would himself come within a hairbreadth of the White House in 1876. "If you wish to be immortal," Van Buren grandly told his youthful protégé, "take this home with you, complete it, revise it, put it into proper shape, and give it to the public."

Tilden did as he was told, further aided in the effort by Van Buren's son John. Soon enough, Democratic lawmakers, goaded ever so deftly by the Red Fox, came out with an endorsement of Van Buren, orchestrated by Van Buren.

In 1848, Van Buren ran on the Free Soil ticket, a third party pledged to oppose slavery. His partisans composed the following ditty to put down Van Buren's opponents, Zachary Taylor and Lewis Cass, as much as to celebrate their own candidate's virtues.

> Come, ye hardy sons of toil,
> And cast your ballots for Free Soil;
> He who'd vote for Zacky Taylor
> Needs a keeper or a jailer.
> And he who for Cass can be
> He is a Cass without the *C*.
> The man on whom we love to look
> Is Martin Van of Kinderhook.

They don't write songs like that anymore.

#37 JAMES BUCHANAN

One of James Buchanan's closest friends summed up this dull, dutiful, indecisive man when he said, "I do not think that he ever uttered a genuine witticism in his life." As president, "the Old Squire" was aided in his social duties by his vivacious niece Harriet Lane, who became something of a celebrity in the process.

(The song "Listen to the Mocking Bird" was dedicated to her.) Characteristically Buchanan advised the lively young woman, "Be quiet and discreet and say nothing."

Such caution may have been useful in diplomatic circles, but it hardly answered the call for bold leadership in a period of national disintegration. In her will Miss Lane left sufficient funds to erect a statue of her uncle—by then all but universally scorned by his countrymen—for no one else would foot the bill.

Something about Buchanan brought out the worst in other people, no one more so than the acerbic Henry Clay. The perennial presidential candidate contrasted the candor of his fellow Whigs with excessive Democratic caution. According to Clay, the heavy guns of the opposition were spiked. "Come out," he cried, "come out like men and define your position. Let us hear from you; I call for the leaders of the party."

Buchanan rose to the bait. Gaining the floor, he denied withholding his opinion on any important issue. Clay was bemused. But it wasn't Buchanan to whom he had been referring, said the Kentuckian. "Far from it. I called for the *leaders* of the party."

Clay was not above making fun of Buchanan for his effete appearance. Once, defending himself against charges of disloyalty in the War of 1812, Buchanan reminded colleagues that when the British had attacked Baltimore, he had joined a company of volunteers.

"You marched to Baltimore?" asked Clay.

He most certainly had, replied Buchanan.

"Armed and equipped?"

Absolutely, said Buchanan.

"But the British had retreated when you arrived," Clay pointed out, and Buchanan nodded in agreement.

"Will the senator from Pennsylvania be good enough to

inform us," said Clay, "whether the British retreated in consequence of his valiantly marching to the relief of Baltimore, or whether he marched to the relief of Baltimore in consequence of the British having already retreated?"

As ambassador to the Court of St. James, Buchanan dispensed with the formal dress of his predecessors. In its place he donned a black coat and trousers, with white waistcoat. To distinguish himself from the upper servants, the American envoy added a plain sword to his sober outfit. "As I approached the Queen," remembered Buchanan, "an arch but benevolent smile lit up her countenance—as much as to say you are the first man who ever appeared before me in court in such a dress. I must confess that I never felt more proud of being an American than when I stood in that brilliant circle in the simple dress of an American citizen."

In fact, Queen Victoria felt anything but benevolent. When a later minister returned to full diplomatic costume, the Queen breathed a sigh of relief. "I am thankful we shall have no more American funerals," she said.

And then there was his fellow Democrat James K. Polk. "Mr. Buchanan is an able man," said Polk, "but in small matters without judgment and sometimes acts like an old maid."

When Polk appointed Buchanan secretary of state, former president Jackson registered a protest of his own. "But, General," replied Polk, "you yourself appointed him minister to Russia."

"Yes, I did," said Jackson. "It was as far as I could send him out of my sight, and where he could do the least harm."

Buchanan's supporters used his nickname to humorous effect during the 1856 campaign:

> We Po'ked 'em in '44,
> We Pierced 'em in '52,
> And we'll "Buck'em" in '56.

Himself a veteran of congressional service, Buchanan was onto something when he advised, "Abstract propositions should never be discussed by a legislative body."

Buchanan's timidity did not extend to press critics. In 1856 he chastised James Gordon Bennett's *New York Herald,* which hated him even more than it liked his Republican opponent John Charles Frémont. "Why am I so traduced and abused by this infamous knave Bennett?" raged Buchanan. "Have I no friends who will visit New York and punish him as he deserves? His ears should be taken off in the public streets!"

Thaddeus Stevens was a master of invective. Buchanan afforded him a worthy object on which to practice. "There is no such person running as James Buchanan," said Stevens in the 1856 campaign. "He is dead of lockjaw. Nothing remains but a platform and a bloated mass of political putridity."

Throughout the nineteenth century, the public was regularly invited inside the White House to shake hands with the chief executive. Buchanan adopted a brisk approach. "Now, gentlemen," he announced at the start of one such reception, "I must take you by the miller's rule, first come, first served. Have the goodness to state your business as shortly as possible, for I have much to do and little time to do it in."

A gracious host, Buchanan was careful to lay in a supply of old JB whiskey for White House entertainments. As a rule, he purchased spirits in ten-gallon casks, going so far as to complain to local merchants when they sent over champagne in small bottles. "Pints are very inconvenient in this house," wrote Buchanan, "as the article is not used in such small quantities."

After a disastrous electoral setback in his home state of Pennsylvania, Buchanan hosted a small dinner party, at which he tried to put things in perspective. "We had a merry time of it," he told his niece later, "laughing among other things over our crushing defeat. It is so great that it is almost absurd."

Asked to sum up Buchanan's performance, Senator John Sherman remarked, "The Constitution provides for every accidental contingency in the executive—except a vacancy in the mind of the president."

On March 4, 1861, Buchanan turned to Abraham Lincoln and piously intoned, "If you are as happy, my dear sir, on entering this house as I am to leave it, you are the happiest man on earth." (This may be the only memorable quote Buchanan ever uttered— and he waited until his last day as president to say it!)

#38 WILLIAM HENRY HARRISON

At the age of twenty, beautiful, willful Anna Symmes enlisted her mother's help and secretly wed a dashing young soldier named William Henry Harrison. Asked by his disapproving father-in-law how he intended to support his bride, Harrison replied, "By my sword, and my own right arm, sir."

Harrison showed rare self-knowledge when he cracked, "Some folks are silly enough as to have formed a plan to make a president of the United States out of this clerk and clodhopper."

The 1840 campaign pitted Harrison, the Log Cabin candidate, against the aristocratic Van Buren. Harrison supporters carried banners contrasting Little Van's policy of "50 cents a day and French soup" against the rugged general, whose election would guarantee "$2 a day and roast beef."

Van Buren had his own opinion of the man who replaced him. "The president of the United States is the most extraordinary man I ever saw," concluded the Red Fox. "He does not seem to realize the vast importance of his elevation. He is as tickled with the presidency as a young woman with a new bonnet."

John Quincy Adams, characteristically, adopted a harsher tone in assessing the new chief executive. Harrison, he concluded, had "an active but shallow mind." The president was "a political adventurer not without talents but self-sufficient, vain, and indiscreet."

On the way to his inaugural, Harrison showed his draft speech to the learned Daniel Webster, who was appalled by its length and preoccupation with the history of ancient Rome. Webster spent an entire day rewriting the turgid prose, with the result that he almost missed a dinner party.

"I hope nothing has gone wrong," said a concerned hostess.

Webster was triumphant. "I have killed seventeen Roman proconsuls as dead as smelts—every one of them!"

As a rule, Webster's displays of classical learning inspired more ridicule than admiration. After one particularly erudite speech, the Scholar in Politics found himself stopped on the streets of New York. "Good morning, Mr. Webster. Recently from Greece, I understand. How did you leave *Mr. Pericles* and *Mr. Aristophanes*?"

Not everyone joined the popular mourning for Harrison. One Democratic newspaper, the *New York Evening Post,* observed tartly that it was unfortunate the Old Hero had not lived "long enough to prove his incapacity for the office of President."

#39 FRANKLIN PIERCE

Pierce was a true child of Congress. "In a body, where there are more than one hundred talking lawyers . . . you can make no calculation upon the termination of any debate and frequently the more trifling the subject the more animated and protracted the discussion."

It cannot be said that Pierce's 1852 nomination produced unbridled joy. His own wife fainted when she heard the news. Nathaniel Hawthorne spoke for many when he told his old friend, "Frank, I pity you—indeed, I do, from the bottom of my heart!" The opposition press had a field day with Pierce's alleged alcoholic tendencies. Making light of his record in the Mexican War, Whig papers declared the Democratic nominee to be the hero of many a well-fought *bottle*.

As one unfriendly New York newspaper put it, "Frank Pierce never made an *effort* in public life that can be recalled without an *effort*."

In his inaugural address, Pierce told his audience, "You have summoned me in my weakness. You must sustain me by your strength." He had it half-right.

Early in his term, a friend of the president's found him signing land patents at the White House. To this acquaintance, at least, Pierce seemed unchanged, exactly "the same free and easy, laughing, and joking Frank Pierce that he always was, and I love him just as well as if he were not president!" The mood was short-lived.

Pierce's fumbling of the slavery issue emboldened critics within his own party. One Mississippi Democrat said of the Pierce administration that it had earned the sneers "of the veriest dolt that chooses to assail it." Looking ahead to 1856, he added, "Unless they mount the Cuban War and ride it in triumph, the whole country will be ready to write *to let* on the door of the White House."

Pierce's support of the Fugitive Slave Law brought a wave of Northern denunciation. In his home state of New Hampshire, the state's chief justice said of Pierce that he had "the damnedest black heart that ever was placed in mortal bosom . . . were he to come into my house, although I should probably treat him with the coldest kind of civility, my toe would feel a great inclination to perform the disagreeable duty of kicking him out!"

One friend declared of Pierce that he was "in rather bad odor, and will stink worse yet before the fourth of next March," when he would leave office. Still, Pierce's friend held the president accountable for the outrages in what was becoming known as Bloody Kansas, "and if he is not called to answer for them here, 'in hell, they'll roast him like a herring.'"

Pierce's enemies could barely wait to hustle him out of office. "I hope he may live to a hale old age," claimed Republican Congressman John Sherman, "and have time to reflect that in politics, as in morals, honesty is the best policy." In fact, Pierce went back to Concord where he drank himself to death.

Leave it to Harry Truman to get to the heart of things. "Pierce was a nincompoop," judged Truman. "He's got the best picture in the White House . . . but being president involves a little bit more than just winning a beauty contest, and he was another one that was a complete fizzle. . . . Pierce didn't know what was going on, and even if he had, he wouldn't have known what to do about it."

#40 BENJAMIN HARRISON

Senators who called upon Harrison found him anything but responsive. As one lawmaker put it, "It's like talking to a hitching post."

Theodore Roosevelt had scant use for Harrison, describing the president as "a cold-blooded, narrow-minded, prejudiced, obstinate, timid old psalm-singing Indianapolis politician."

A Harrison supporter urged House Speaker Reed to get on the president's bandwagon. "Bandwagon, hell," proclaimed Reed, "it is nothing but a damned old Presbyterian icewagon." In the litany of presidential temperaments, it would be said that Grant, the soldier, drilled his visitors out of his office; that Hayes, the great champion of temperance, dried them out; that Garfield preached them out; and that Harrison froze them out.

During the Civil War, Harrison distinguished himself on the battlefield, eventually attaining the rank of brigadier general. This was all the more impressive since Harrison made plain his lack of military ambition. In his own words, "I am a plain Hoosier colonel with no more relish for a fight than for a good breakfast and hardly so much."

It might have amazed his fellow politicians, but before an audience of newspapermen, Benjamin Harrison could be downright funny. Harrison was the first president to speak before Washington's venerable Gridiron Club. Making a subtle reference to journalistic credibility, Harrison told his audience that it was the second time that week he had been called upon to open a congress of American inventors.

At the conclusion of another humorous address, an unfriendly journalist turned to a White House confidant. "Your man Harrison is a wonder," said the erstwhile critic. "I didn't think it was in him."

"Oh, he's all right on his feet," came the reply. "It's only when he sits down that he falls down."

Harry Truman lumped Harrison together with Dwight Eisenhower as the two presidents who most preferred laziness to labor.

During the 1888 campaign, Republicans were embarrassed by apparent vote-buying sanctioned by the party's treasurer, W. W. Dudley. A letter, allegedly from Dudley's pen, surfaced shortly before election day. "Divide the voters into blocks of five," it read, "and put a trusted man with the necessary funds in charge of these five, and make him responsible that none get away and that all vote our ticket." Harrison was furious with the man forever after known as Blocks of Five Dudley.

Harrison was less than cordial in his relations with other politicians. The governor of Ohio arrived for an appointment, only to find the president with a watch in his hand and a massive pile of reports on his desk. "I've got all these papers to look after," said Harrison, "and I'm going fishing at two o'clock." At which point the president opened his watch case and waited for the visitor to transact his business.

Ike Hoover, for forty years a mainstay of the White House staff, began his career overseeing newly installed electric lights. The job was more demanding than it sounds, given that President Harrison and his family refused to turn on any light for fear of electrocution. In fact, the president shied away from electric buttons used to summon servants.

One evening a White House steward appeared in the East Room to announce a state dinner. One leg of his trousers was up, leaving his long underwear clearly visible. The next day Mrs. Harrison casually asked the elderly servant if he had adopted the English style for his breeches. And if he had, she wondered, then why did it only apply to one leg?

Many of Harrison's political problems stemmed from restlessness among Western Republicans who disagreed with him over the gold standard. Half a dozen states joined the Union during the Harrison administration, yet the president saw only new votes for the coinage of Western silver. As he put it wryly, "I wish this free coinage of senators would stop."

Even Harrison's intimates took care to avoid the president's famous temper. His executive secretary, Elijah Halford, said as much to reporters. "When I see him in the morning and he greets me with 'Halford, how are you today?' I sit down by his desk for a pleasant talk about matters. When he greets me with 'Good morning, Mr. Halford,' I bolt the door and wait until after lunch for the talk."

A low point of the Harrison administration came in the summer of 1890, when newspaper reports suggested irregularities in the construction of a New Jersey beachfront cottage as a summer White House. Soon audiences were being treated to a Gilbert-and-Sullivan-style parody:

> The president said a vacation he did take;
> Said he to himself, said he,
> Down by the blue sea, where the high breakers break,
> Said he to himself, said he;
> For the place needed the boom that my presence will bring,
> And my friends who belong to the real estate ring
> Have promised a cottage, to which I shall cling;
> Said he to himself, said he.

As late as 1960, Democratic orators were still having a field day with Harrison. In his campaign that year, John F. Kennedy recounted the legend of Harrison encountering a man forced by economic hardship to eat grass on the White House lawn. As Kennedy told it, the president had only one suggestion for his unwanted visitor—he should go around to the back lawn where the grass was longer.

#41 MILLARD FILLMORE

As vice president, Fillmore was called upon to rebuke senators who regularly pinched snuff from two large containers atop the presiding officer's desk. Other lawmakers resorted to wine or spirits to stimulate the flow of debate. Worst of all, said the well-meaning Fillmore, "A practice seems to have grown up of interrupting a senator when speaking, by addressing him directly, instead of addressing the chair, as required by the rule." If only Fillmore could see today's lawmakers.

As a candidate for Congress, Fillmore picked up his morning mail to find a questionnaire from a local antislavery society. It asked his opinion on the right of citizens to petition their representatives on slavery and the slave trade; the annexation of Texas; the immediate abolition of slavery in the District of Columbia; and other inflammatory subjects.

"The Philistines are upon us," said Fillmore. Later, when he cooled off, he answered the questionnaire in the affirmative.

"He is miserable whose happiness 'hangs on a prince's favors,'" Fillmore once lamented, "but he is not only wretched, but infinitely degraded whose means of support depends on the wild caprice of the ever-changing multitude." Apparently no one ever told Fillmore that the multitude and its wild caprices go by the name of popular democracy.

Believe it or not, in 1844 Fillmore actually wanted to be vice president. His opponents in New York State wanted to head him off by dangling the governorship before him. "I receive letters," he told a friend, "from my friends in various parts of the state, stating that Governor Seward's most intimate friends are *killing me with kindness* . . . but I do not suppose for a moment that I think they desire my nomination for governor."

The election of James K. Polk in 1844 sent Fillmore into despair. "May God save the country," he wrote gloomily, "for it is evident that the people will not."

Not surprisingly for a man from Buffalo, Fillmore paid a great deal of attention to commerce on the Great Lakes. He was especially disappointed when John Tyler vetoed a program for river and harbor improvements sure to stimulate trade across the border. He found it incredible that "these ponds! Lake Erie and Lake Ontario, and Lake Huron, and even Lake Superior cannot be taken under the care of the Constitution."

For himself, "I believe the Constitution is not a saltwater animal . . . it can live as well in fresh as in salt water."

For a man whose chief objective in life was pacifying opposites, Millard Fillmore inspired an unusual amount of criticism. So intense were the attacks on the president by his fellow Whigs that William Seward likened them to a series of sermons he had once heard: "Hell—more Hell—still more Hell."

As an ex-president, Fillmore flirted with the American, or Know-Nothing, Party—a nativist organization whose popular name stemmed, not, as one might suspect, from its policies, but from its semisecret rituals. Eager to return to the White House in 1856, Fillmore embarked on a campaign tour of the South. Author Washington Irving begged off from accompanying him. "I have no inclination to travel with political notorieties," said Irving, "to be smothered by the clouds of party dust whirled up by their chariot wheels, and beset by the speechmakers and little great men and bores of every community."

Restless as ever, Fillmore soon after left for a European excursion—odd, given that few Europeans voted in American elections. For those who inquired the reason behind his constant travels, Fillmore had a ready explanation: "It is better to wear out than rust out, and as my political life has unfortunately deprived me of my profession, perhaps I could do nothing better than to diversify my pursuits by traveling."

Fillmore wasn't altogether comfortable visiting Oxford University. Publicly he explained his declination of an honorary degree by saying, "I had not the advantage of a classical education, and no man should, in my judgment, accept a degree he cannot read." In private, however, he feared a demonstration by unruly students. "They would probably ask, 'Who's Fillmore? What's he done? Where did he come from?' And then my name would . . . give them an excellent opportunity to make jokes at my expense."

"It is a national disgrace that our presidents . . . should be cast adrift, and perhaps be compelled to keep a corner grocery for subsistence," said Fillmore out of office. "We elect a man to the presidency, expect him to be honest, to give up a lucrative profession, perhaps, and after we have done with him, we let him go into seclusion and perhaps poverty." Not to worry; Fillmore had a solution–a $12,000 annual pension for former presidents. It was one of those rare instances when he was ahead of his times. If Fillmore had proposed a pension for losing presidential candidates, I might have rated him a little higher.

Waiting in the Wings

America's forty-third president takes the oath of office on January 20, 2001. While Campaign 2000 was probably not the funniest campaign in American history, it certainly was the closest. And as this book goes to print, the candidates and the nation are awaiting the verdict of the voters. While only one of the candidates will serve as America's forty-third president, perhaps the losing candidate can take heart in the fact that I have included examples of his wit in this book.

GEORGE W. BUSH

During the campaign for the Republican nomination for president in 2000, Bush quipped, "If you want to get rid of pork in Washington, stop feeding the hogs."

When opponents have difficulty finding issues on which they disagree fundamentally, someone has to dig to the root of the issue. In the 1978 congressional race, Bush and his Democratic opponent, Kent Hance, faced such a challenge. According to the *Reporter-Telegram,* the two men were asked to explain what, if any, were the differences between them.

After taking some time to think through the question, Bush replied, "Well, I've got more hair."

Responding to speculation and comments about his father's involvement in his campaign, Bush said, "The man is not a political consultant. He's a father."

"Can you imagine how much it hurt to know that Dad's idea of the perfect son was Al Gore?" Bush once said jokingly before a crowd.

Assessing polls in his favor with a glass is half-full and half-empty attitude, Bush said of one July 2000 poll, "The good news is we're ahead in the polls. The bad news is the election isn't tomorrow."

Poking a barb at President Bill Clinton's convoluted explanation of his testimony in the Paula Jones case, Bush said this about Dick Cheney, his vice-presidential running mate: "I picked a man from Wyoming and I made a great pick in Dick Cheney. The West is a place of straightforward people, a place where people understand what the meaning of the word 'is' is."

"You know about my abstinence program?" Bush asked, referring to his efforts to encourage sexual abstinence among Texas teens. "We have not extended that to the agricultural world," he added, while talking about cattle production.

Throughout the Republican primaries, Bush and his campaign proudly promulgated every endorsement they received. In early

May 2000, Bush took this trumpeting of endorsements quite literally to the outer limits. He showed reporters in the back of his campaign plane a spread in the tabloid *Weekly World News* that featured a photograph of Bush shaking hands with a reptilian space alien. The accompanying article was headlined, "Space Alien Backs Bush for President!" Bush noted dryly that his alien encounter was further proof of his commitment to expanding the Republican Party's appeal. "New faces, new voices," he said, brandishing the headline. "It goes to show I'm willing to reach across certain demographic lines."

Bush once gave an audience an interesting take on the old saying about the pot and the kettle: "Don't be taking a speck out of your neighbor's eye, when you got a log in your own," he said.

Bush's wit was even more honed on *The Tonight Show with Jay Leno* a few days later, where he discussed his late father-in-law. "He was a good West Texas man. . . . They lowered their standards and let me into the family."

Leno asked Bush, "When you were out at a frat party, having a good time at Yale partying with the boys, were you ever thinking, 'You know, I don't want to have that beer. I might be running for president.' Did that ever cross your mind?"

Bush deadpanned: "No."

After Leno's persistent questions about Bush's reputation as a cheapskate, Bush turned the joke around against the multimillion-dollar TV star.

"Well, I'm thrifty. I'm going to be tight with your money—all that money you make," Bush said.

Leno asked Bush whether he'd gotten tired of those tricky world leader questions that tripped him up early in his campaign.

"Naaaah," Bush replied. "Let me say something about that

world leader deal. My mother raised me not to show off, and I didn't let her down."

In July 2000, he talked with the press corps on board his campaign plane. "I don't read half of what you write," he admitted.

"We don't listen to half of what you say," one of the reporters retorted.

"That's apparent in the other half of what I read," Bush replied quickly.

When asked what he would say in his acceptance speech at the Republican Convention, Bush quipped, "I thought I would start off with 'I accept your nomination.' It might not be very original, but it seems to get a good applause."

Early in his acceptance speech, Bush lightened the tone considerably by saying, "Together, we will renew America's purpose. Our founders first defined that purpose here in Philadelphia. Ben Franklin was here. Thomas Jefferson. And, of course, George Washington—or, as his friends called him, 'George W.'"

He spoke of his beloved mother, Barbara: "Growing up, she gave me love and lots of advice. I gave her white hair."

While he conceded in his speech that the retirement system is "the third rail of politics, the one you're not supposed to touch because it shocks you," he also said, "But if you don't touch it, you can't fix it. And I intend to fix it."

Bush pointed out in his acceptance speech that some of his proposals—including tax cuts, private retirement accounts, a missile defense system—had been called "risky schemes" by Gore. Bush said, "If my opponent had been at the moon launch, it would have been a risky rocket scheme. If he had been there when Edison was testing the light bulb, it would have been a risky anti-candle scheme. And if he'd been there when the Internet was invented, well . . . I understand he actually was there for that."

AL GORE

Debating former football captain and vice-presidential hopeful Jack Kemp in St. Petersburg, Gore began: "I'd like to start by offering you a deal, Jack. If you won't use any . . . football stories, I won't tell any of my warm and humorous stories about . . . chlorofluorocarbon abatement."

In his 1994 keynote speech to several thousand California delegates, Gore recalled some amusing quips made about his stiff demeanor: "'He's so stiff, racks buy their suits off Al Gore.' 'If you use a strobe light, it looks like Al Gore is actually moving.' 'Al Gore is an inspiration to millions of Americans who suffer from Dutch elm disease.'"

"I've heard 'em all," Gore told the delighted crowd, "and each time I say, 'Very funny, Tipper.'"

When Gore's father, Senator Albert Gore Sr., died in December 1998, Gore gave the heartfelt eulogy, which many consider one of the finest speeches of his entire career. He remembered his father's wit: "He loved practical jokes. His humor often had an edge. One Saturday night in the early 1930s, at a party he organized in a barn by the Cumberland River for a group of friends in Carthage, he planted the suggestion that quite a few rattlesnakes had been seen in the area the preceding day. Surreptitiously, in the shadows thrown by the fire, he attached a fishhook to the pant leg of his friend Walter Merryman. At the other end of the hook was tied a large blacksnake he had killed in the barn before the party guests arrived. Rejoining the circle, he bided his time for a moment, and then suddenly pointed toward Merryman's leg and shouted, "Snake!" The more Merryman jumped and ran, the more determined the pursuing snake appeared. The prank worked a little too well, when the fishhook dug into Merryman's calf. Certain that it was a rattlesnake's fang, he collapsed in fear. It took several months for the friendship to be repaired, but the story became such a local legend, that someone told me about it again last night at the wake."

Toward the end of the eulogy, Gore remembered, "Two years ago, when he was eighty-nine, [my father] was still driving his car. I had great difficulty persuading him to stop. When I asked my friends and neighbors in Carthage to help, one of them said, 'Oh, don't worry, Al. We know his car. We just get off the road when we see him coming.'"

Much has been made of Gore telling CNN that he "invented the Internet." (The precise quote: He told Wolf Blitzer, "During my service in the United States Congress, I took the initiative in creating the Internet.") His explanation: "The day I made that comment, I was tired from staying up all night inventing the camcorder."

Gore frequently tells a joke about a man who went out driving when he was tired, which worried his wife. The woman was listening to the radio, and heard that a driver was posing a risk to other motorists by driving the wrong way on the highway. Concerned about his safety, she called her husband on his cell phone to tell him. "It's worse than that, honey!" the man told her. "There's hundreds of 'em!"

In early May, months before his choice of Senator Joe Lieberman as his running mate, Gore spoke before the Anti-Defamation League. He tried out a Borscht Belt routine before the largely Jewish audience. He told the audience that a subgenre of music was proliferating in Nashville: The Jewish Country-Western song.

Reaching number four on the charts, he said, was "I Was One of the Chosen People–Until She Chose Somebody Else." Number three: "The Second Time She Said 'Shalom,' I Knew She Meant Good-bye." Number two: "I've Got My Foot on the Glass, Now Where Are You?" And number one, which Gore actually sang with a soft lilt and a twang, "Mommas, Don't Let Your Ungrateful Sons Grow Up to Be Cowboys When They Could Very Easily Just Have Taken Over the Family Business That My Own Grandfather Broke His Back to Start and My Father Sweated Over the Years, Which Apparently Doesn't Mean Anything Now That You're Turning Your Back on Such a Gift."

Gore told the audience at the Columbia Law School commencement in May 2000, "I'm grateful for this chance to talk with you just before you graduate. I understand that right after the ceremony, this conversation will cost me two hundred dollars an hour."

"Now these days," he said a bit later, "some find it fashionable to bash the legal profession. I'm sure that by now, you've heard all those lawyer jokes.

"You know, like the one about the shark that won't eat the lawyer out of professional courtesy.

"Actually, somebody pointed out that there's a big, basic, generic problem with all lawyer jokes. Lawyers don't think they're funny, and nobody else thinks they're jokes."

Gore's appearance on *The Late Show with David Letterman* on September 14, 2000, included the inevitable "Top Ten List" segment, for which Gore provided comical "rejected campaign slogans." They were:

10. Vote for me or I'll come to your home and explain my 191-page economic plan to you in excruciating detail.

9. Remember, America, I gave you the Internet and I can take it away. Think about it.

8. Your vote automatically enters you in a drawing for the $123 billion surplus.

7. With Lieberman on the ticket, you get all kinds of fun new days off. Vote for us, we're going to work 24/6.

6. We know when the microphone is on.

5. Vote for me and I will take whatever steps are necessary to outlaw the term "Whazzzup."

4. Gore-Lieberman: You don't have to worry about pork-barrel politics.

3. You'll thank us in four years when the escalator to the moon is finished.

2. If I can handle Letterman, I can handle Saddam Hussein.

1. I'll be twice as cool as that president guy in the West Wing.